Uncover 1

Workbook
with Digital Pack

Susan Evento

CAMBRIDGE
UNIVERSITY PRESS

DISCOVERY
EDUCATION

Shaftesbury Road, Cambridge CB2 8EA, United Kingdom

One Liberty Plaza, 20th Floor, New York, NY 10006, USA

477 Williamstown Road, Port Melbourne, VIC 3207, Australia

314–321, 3rd Floor, Plot 3, Splendor Forum, Jasola District Centre, New Delhi – 110025, India

103 Penang Road, #05–06/07, Visioncrest Commercial, Singapore 238467

Cambridge University Press & Assessment is a department of the University of Cambridge.

We share the University's mission to contribute to society through the pursuit of education, learning and research at the highest international levels of excellence.

www.cambridge.org
Information on this title: www.cambridge.org/9781107493070

First published 2015

40 39 38 37 36 35 34 33 32 31 30 29 28 27 26 25 24

Printed in Great Britain by Ashford Colour Press Ltd.

A catalog record for this publication is available from the British Library.

ISBN 978-1-107-49307-0 Workbook with Digital Pack 1

Additional resources for this publication at www.cambridge.org/uncover

Art direction, book design, layout services, and photo research: QBS Learning

Table of Contents

1 Welcome Back!

Classroom objects and colors

1 Circle nine more classroom objects.

chairboardnotebookpencilbookshelfdictionaryeraserrulerbackpackbook

2 Complete the sentences with color words.

1. Black + white = _____gray_____

2. Red + blue = _____

3. Blue + yellow = _____

4. Red + yellow = _____

5. Red + yellow + blue = _____

3 Complete the sentences with color words.

1. The American flag is red, white, and ____blue____.

2. The sun is a big _____ ball.

3. Most soccer balls are _____ and white.

4. The angry boy's face is _____.

5. Snow is _____.

4 Answer the questions.

1. What color is your notebook?

_____*My notebook is black.*_____

2. What color is your pencil?

_____

3. What color are your eyes?

_____

4. What colors are your schoolbooks?

_____

5. What color are your shoes?

_____

6. What color is your backpack?

_____

GRAMMAR Simple present of *be* and subject pronouns

1 Circle the correct simple present forms of *be*.

1. I **is** / **am** a good photographer.

2. He **is** / **am** a new student.

3. They **is** / **are** good friends.

4. It **is** / **are** Tuesday.

5. We **are** / **is** at the store.

6. She **am** / **is** happy it is Friday.

7. You **are** / **is** next in line.

8. Brett and Jim **is** / **are** football players.

9. The band **are** / **is** playing.

10. That team **is** / **are** the best.

2 Complete the sentences with the correct pronouns.

1. Betty is in the band. _____*She*_____ isn't a dancer.

2. My friend and I are in middle school. _____ aren't in high school.

3. Brian and Justin are in different grades. _____ aren't in the same classes.

4. The dictionary is on the bookshelf. _____ isn't on the desk.

5. Jim is in the library. _____ isn't in the cafeteria.

3 Complete the chart. Use contractions.

	Affirmative	Negative	Question
I	I am in this class.	*I'm not in this class.*	
He		He isn't angry.	
She			Is she a musician?
It		It isn't a nice day.	
You	You are at the party.		
We			Are we early for the show?
They		They aren't home now.	

4 Correct the verbs.

     are
1. They ~~is~~ in the same class.

2. Are he on the football team?

3. I is not angry with you.

4. John and I am best friends.

5. It am Tuesday.

6. The team are at the field.

7. What are his favorite class?

8. Who is your classmates?

5 Answer the questions.

1. How old are you?

   _____

2. Who are your best friends?

   _____

3. Are you on a team? What team?

   _____

   _____

4. What is your favorite color?

   _____

5. Who are your favorite bands?

   _____

VOCABULARY Instructions

1 Put the letters in the correct order to make words.

1. AERD _____read_____

2. RNTU _____

3. MCOE _____

4. PONE _____

5. SEAIR _____

6. TISENL _____

7. SATND _____

8. OSLCE _____

9. IST _____

2 Write the instructions under the pictures. Use the verbs. Some instructions use nouns.

Verbs	Nouns
be quiet	~~the article~~
close	the book
open	the door
~~read~~	your name
sit down	
stand up	
write	

1. _Read the article._   2. _____

3. _____   4. _____

5. _____   6. _____

3 Write three more instructions. Use words from Exercises 1 and 2.

1. _____ _Open the window._ _____

2. _____

3. _____

4. _____

4 Where do you hear the instructions? Circle the correct answers.

1. Open your book.

   a. at home

   b. at school

   c. at the gym

2. Be quiet.

   a. in the cafeteria

   b. in the library

   c. in the park

3. Raise your hand.

   a. at home

   b. in the park

   c. in the classroom

4. Listen to the teacher.

   a. at school

   b. at home

   c. on the football field

5. Turn to page 12.

   a. in the gym

   b. in the cafeteria

   c. in the classroom

6. Close the window.

   a. at home

   b. on the football field

   c. in the park

1 Correct the sentences.

HOUSEHOLD RULES

1. Leave your clothes on the floor.

   Don't leave your clothes on the floor.

2. Be loud at the dinner table.

   _____

   _____

3. Don't get up when your alarm rings in the morning.

   _____

   _____

4. Don't go to bed early.

   _____

   _____

5. Fight with your brother and sister.

   _____

   _____

6. Don't do your homework.

   _____

   _____

7. Play soccer in the house.

   _____

   _____

8. Don't turn off the lights when you leave the room.

   _____

   _____

2 Rewrite the sentences. Use _please_ to make the commands softer. Remember, _please_ can go at the beginning or end of a sentence.

1. Don't go in the street.

   _____ _Please don't go in the street._ _____ OR

   _____ _Don't go in the street, please._ _____

2. Don't say that again.

   _____

3. Sit down.

   _____

4. Take turns.

   _____

5. Look at this.

   _____

6. Don't write in the book.

   _____

7. Be quiet in the library.

   _____

8. Don't eat in class.

   _____

3 Complete the sentences with imperatives.

be	listen	raise	stand
eat	open	sit	turn

1. _____ _Eat_ _____ your vegetables. They are good for you.

2. _____ the window to let air in.

3. _____ your hand to talk.

4. Please _____ to what I say.

5. It's dark. _____ the light on.

6. Don't _____ on the desk.

7. Don't _____ on the chairs. It's dangerous.

8. Please _____ on time for class.

CONVERSATION   That's my name!

1 Put the words in the correct order to make questions or sentences. Then complete the conversation.

do / say / that word / How / you /

repeat / Can / that / you /

does / mean / that word / what /

understand / don't / I /

Juan: Hey, Marisa.

Marisa: Hey, Juan. Look at this book.

¹ *How do you say that word* ?

Juan: "Board."

Marisa: ² _____ slowly, please?

Juan: Sure. "Board."

Marisa: Thanks, but ³ _____ ?

Juan: It's something the teacher writes on.

Marisa: Huh? ⁴ _____ .

Juan: Ms. Wilson writes our lessons on the board.

Marisa: Oh. Now I understand! Thanks. I like to learn new words.

2 Use the words to complete the conversation. There are two extra words.

| How | repeat | understand |
| mean | say | What |

Luc: Hey, Juan.

Juan: Hi, Luc.

Luc: ¹ _____ do you say *bonjour* in English?

Juan: *Hello.*

Luc: I don't ² _____ . How do you spell it?

Juan: H-E-L-L-O.

Luc: Can you ³ _____ that, please?

Juan: Sure. H-E-L-L-O.

Luc: Oh, *hello*. Thanks.

Juan: Hey, Luc. What does *notebook* ⁴ _____ ?

Luc: Oh, I know that word. It's a book you write in.

Juan: I need to buy one of those.

1 Match the pictures with the sentences. Then add one Do rule to the list and one Don't rule.

POOL RULES: DOS AND DON'TS

Do . . .

1. ____*b*____ Wear a bathing cap.

2. _____ Be safe on the diving board!

3. _____ Take a shower before you go in the pool.

4. _____
   _____

Don't . . .

1. _____ Don't play loud music.

2. _____ Don't run!

3. _____ Don't eat or drink in the pool.

4. _____
   _____

2 Read the instructions for riding a bike. Add missing periods and exclamation points.

1. Wear a helmet

2. Use lights at night

3. Hold the handlebars

4. Look both ways before you turn

5. Stop at the red light

3 Think of a game or activity that has important rules. Write four Do rules and four Don't rules. Write the most important rules first. Add periods or exclamation points.

_____

Dos	**Don'ts**
_____	_____
_____	_____
_____	_____
_____	_____

2 My World

Personal items

1 Complete the crossword puzzle.

Down

1.   2.

4.   5.

7.   8.

Across

3.   6.   7.

9.   10.   11.

2 Look at Selena Gomez's favorite things. Complete her profile with the correct words.

comic books
soccer
guitar
tablet
sneakers

My Favorite Things

by Selena

Favorite sport: _____ *soccer* _____

Favorite technology: _____

Favorite things to read: _____

Favorite instrument: _____

Favorite shoes: _____

3 Complete the sentences with the correct words.

guitar	skateboard
inline skates	soccer ball
laptop	tablet
~~MP3 player~~	sneakers

1. We use an _____ *MP3 player* _____ and a _____ to play music.

2. A _____ and a _____ are types of computers.

3. People wear _____ and _____ on their feet.

4. Paul likes to kick a _____, but John likes to ride a _____

GRAMMAR Possessives

1 Complete the sentences with possessive adjectives.

Subject pronouns	Possessive adjectives
I	I like _____*my*_____ pink hat.
you	Eat _____ vegetables.
he	He meets _____ mother at the store.
she	She plays _____ favorite song.
it	See that lake? _____ name is Lake Erie.
we	We eat _____ lunch together on Fridays.
you	Please tell me _____ names.
they	Jan and Kim meet _____ friends at the store.

2 Complete the sentences with possessive adjectives.

1. My family has a cat. _____*Our*_____ cat's name is Josie.

2. Carlos is from Italy. _____ family is from Rome.

3. Two students in the class don't have _____ homework.

4. We have many students in _____ school.

5. That dress is very pretty. _____ colors are beautiful.

6. You have to do _____ homework!

3 Rewrite the sentences. Use possessive adjectives.

1. The students' teacher is very nice!

_____*Their teacher is very nice!*_____

2. Stephanie's parents are doctors.

_____

3. Dave talks to Dave's grandmother on the phone every week.

_____

4. Shawn and my friend is from Ireland.

_____

5. Caroline's brothers and sisters are in a band.

_____

4 Complete the sentences with possessive adjectives or name/noun + 's or s'.

Laia   Alicia

Hector   Sergio

1. _____*Laia's*_____ favorite thing is _____*her*_____ cat, Chester.

2. _____ favorite thing is _____ game console.

3. _____ favorite thing is _____ guitar.

4. _____ favorite things are _____ books.

5 Circle the correct words.

1. The **boy's /(boys')** names **is / are** James and Connor.

2. The two **girl's / girls'** favorite game **is / are** soccer.

3. My **teacher's / teachers'** names **is / are** Mr. Kent and Ms. Childs.

4. The **truck's / trucks'** engine **is / are** loud.

5. All of the **student's / students'** papers **is / are** interesting.

6 Correct the sentences.

1. My brothers name is Sam.

_____*My brother's name is Sam.*_____

2. Lauras favorite color is red.

_____

3. Carlos loves its cat.

_____

4. The cars colors are black and blue.

_____

5. We do her homework together.

_____

VOCABULARY Countries, nationalities, and languages

1 Put the letters in the correct order to make words.

1. GUORPTEESU _Portuguese_

2. GISHLEN _____

3. ISHANSP _____

4. ALITIAN _____

5. IABRZILAN _____

6. NEIXMCA _____

7. DIAANNAC _____

8. SEPAJANE _____

2 Match the countries with the nationalities.

1. Japan   a. Mexican
2. Australia   b. British
3. Brazil   c. Australian
4. Mexico   d. Brazilian
5. the UK   e. French
6. France   f. Japanese

3 Complete the sentences with the correct languages.

1. Spanish people speak _____Spanish_____.

2. Canadians speak English and _____.

3. Sudanese people speak English and _____.

4. Australians speak _____.

5. Brazilians speak _____.

6. British people speak _____.

7. In Colombia, people speak _____.

8. In Italy, people speak _____.

4 Write the nationalities and languages.

Penelope Cruz   Taylor Swift

Robert Pattinson   Keith Urban

Cristiano Ronaldo   Sofia Vegara

1. Penelope Cruz is from Spain. She's _____Spanish_____. She speaks _____.

2. Taylor Swift is from America. She's _____. She speaks _____.

3. Robert Pattinson is from the U.K. He's _____. He speaks _____.

4. Keith Urban is from Australia. He's _____. He speaks _____.

5. Cristiano Ronaldo is from Portugal. He's _____. He speaks _____.

6. Sofia Vegara is from Colombia. She's _____. She speaks _____.

5 Choose three people. Write sentences about their nationalities and the languages they speak.

1. _____

_____

2. _____

_____

3. _____

_____

1 Read the paragraph. Then circle the correct question words. Answer the questions.

Juan lives in Puerto Rico. He goes to Antilles Middle School. Juan takes English, math, science, history, and computer lab. He has two best friends. They are Luis and Edwin. On Fridays, they walk or ride their bicycles to the park. They play baseball at the park. It is their favorite sport.

1. **How / (Where)** does Juan live?

He lives in Puerto Rico.

2. **Where / What** does he go to school?

_____

3. **What / Where** are his classes in school?

_____

4. **How / Who** are his best friends?

_____

5. **When / Where** do they go to the park?

_____

6. **What / How** do the boys get to the park?

_____

7. **When / What** sport do the boys play at the park?

_____

2 Fill in the correct question words. Then answer the questions.

1. _____What_____ is your name?

_____

2. _____ do you live?

_____

3. _____ old are you?

_____

4. _____ is your birthday?

_____

5. _____ class are you in?

_____

6. _____ do you get to school?

_____

7. _____ are your favorite things to do?

_____

8. _____ are your favorite classes?

_____

3 Read the answers. Write the questions.

Hello, my name is Asako!

1. _____ _Where are you from?_ _____

I'm from Tokyo, Japan.

2. _____

My best friends are Kameko and Nami.

3. _____

My English teacher is Mr. Smith.

4. _____

My favorite thing is my MP3 player!

1 Put the sentences in order to make a conversation.

Marty: Hello! My name is Marty. What's your name?

Marty: Nice to meet you, too.

Josh: Are you the new player on our soccer team?

Marty: Yes, I am.

Marty: Thanks! Hey, I've got class. See you on the soccer field. Bye!

Josh: That's great. Welcome to the team.

Josh: Hi. My name's Josh. Nice to meet you.

2 Circle the correct words.

1. **This** / **That** is my mother next to me. **These** / **Those** are her friends Mr. and Mrs. Miller right next to her.

2. **That** / **This** is my brother on the soccer field. And **these** / **those** are his friends with him.

3. Come meet one of my best friends. **This** / **That** is Marcia.

4. **These** / **Those** people near the door are Marcia's family.

1 Read Amaris Moreno's profile. Complete the chart.

My name is Amaris Moreno. I'm Colombian and I'm from Bogotá. I live with my mom and dad. We all speak English and Spanish.

I am 11 years old. My birthday is in just a few days, on April 15. I can't wait for my party with my favorite music and food. I love rap music and pizza.

My favorite thing to do is play my guitar. I also like to write stories and play games on my new tablet.

Name	Birthday / Age
Amaris Moreno	
Town / City	**Country**
Nationality	**Languages**
Likes	**Interests**

2 Correct the incorrect words. Add capital letters. Then use the words to write four sentences about Adriano.

     S
1. Adriano ~~s~~ilva, são Paulo, brazil

    His name is Adriano Silva, and he lives in São Paulo, Brazil.

2. brazilian, Portuguese

_____.

3. Birthday: may 3

_____

4. Favorite soccer player: victor andrade

_____

1 Label each object. Then circle the classroom words.

board	game console	ruler
comic books	inline skates	skateboard
dictionary	notebook	soccer ball
eraser	pencil	

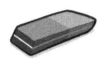 

1. _____ 2. _____

3. _____ 4. _____

5. _____ 6. _____

7. _____ 8. _____

9. _____ 10. _____

11. _____

2 Fill in the correct words.

1. Jason is from Australia. He is _____.
   He speaks _____.

2. Elena is from _____. She is Brazilian.
   She speaks _____.

3. Mateo is from Spain. He is _____.
   He speaks _____.

4. Samir is from Sudan. He is _____.
   He speaks _____ and English.

5. Amaya is from Japan. She is _____.
   She speaks _____.

6. Eduardo is from Colombia. He is _____.
   He speaks _____.

3 Complete the sentences with the correct form of be.

1. The pencil _____ yellow.

2. John and Pat _____ in my class.

3. Our school band _____ new.

4. I _____ a football player on our school team.

5. Tryouts _____ tomorrow.

6. The ruler and the eraser _____ pink.

4 Make the sentences in Exercise 3 negative. Use subject pronouns for names and objects. Use contractions.

1. _____ *It isn't yellow.* _____

2. _____

3. _____

4. _____

5. _____

6. _____

5 Complete the class rules handout with the imperative form of the verbs.

be	open	read	sit
come	raise	run	talk

Welcome to
AMERICAN HISTORY!
Please follow this list of class rules.

Dos:

1. _____ your hand in class. Questions are good!

2. _____ on time. Class starts at 1:30.

3. _____ to every class.

4. _____ your book for homework.

Don'ts:

1. _____ in the hall.

2. _____ when your teacher or classmates are talking.

3. _____ on your desk. Use your chair.

4. _____ your books during tests.

6 Use a possessive adjective or a name/noun + 's or s' for plural subjects.

1. (Lily) _____ game console is _____ favorite thing.

2. (Anuj) _____ favorite thing is _____ dog, Rusty.

3. The (girls) _____ favorite things are _____ MP3 players.

4. The new (students) _____ names are Zack and Ian, and _____ teacher is Mrs. Lucas.

7 Ask and answer questions about Pedro.

Pedro's Personal Profile	★ Bogota
Name	Pedro Alonzez
Age	12
Birthday	4/15
Nationality	Colombian
Town/City	Bogotá
Country	Colombia
Language(s)	Spanish
Interests/ Favorite things	Soccer, rap music

1. **A:** _____
   B: He lives in Bogotá, Colombia.

2. **A:** _____
   B: Pedro is 12 years old.

3. **A:** What is Pedro's favorite sport?
   B: _____

4. **A:** What kind of music does Pedro like?
   B: _____

5. **A:** What language does Pedro speak?
   B: _____

6. **A:** _____
   B: It is April 15.

8 Complete the meeting and greeting conversations with the words in the box.

fine	problem
later	welcome
meet	what's
name	you

1. **A:** My _____ is Alex. _____ your name?
   B: I'm Paola.

2. **A:** Nice to _____ you!
   B: Nice to meet you, too!

3. **A:** Where are you from?
   B: I'm from the USA. And what about _____?

4. **A:** How are you?
   B: _____ thanks, and you?

5. **A:** Thanks for your help!
   B: No _____. You're _____.

6. **A:** See you at 3:00.
   B: See you _____.

9 Put the words in the correct order to ask questions about learning a new language. Then match the questions to the answers.

1. please / repeat / that / you / Can / ?
   _____
   _____

2. spell / do / English / in / you / How / *diccionario* / ?
   _____
   _____

3. don't / I / understand /.
   _____
   _____

4. mean / What / it / does / ?
   _____
   _____

a. I'll try to explain.

b. It is a book that tells you what words mean.

c. D-I-C-T-I-O-N-A-R-Y

d. Yes, the word is *dictionary*.

3 People in My Life

1 Look at the family tree. Circle the correct family words.

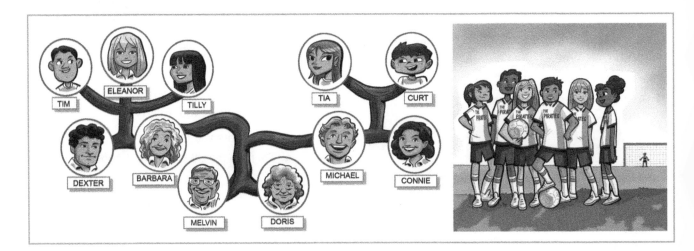

1. Barbara is Eleanor's **mother** / **aunt**.

2. Tia and Curt are her **parents** / **cousins**.

3. Melvin is her **uncle** / **grandfather**.

4. Michael is her **cousin** / **uncle**.

5. Connie is her **sister** / **aunt**.

6. Eleanor is Melvin's and Doris's **son** / **granddaughter**.

7. Dexter and Barbara are her **parents** / **grandparents**.

8. "The Pirates" are Eleanor's **classmates** / **teammates**.

2 Find 12 more words for friends and family.

S	T	T	R	M	Y	P	W	D	A	T	N	F
E	A	N	C	O	U	S	I	N	T	E	K	O
F	H	U	L	T	U	B	N	R	Q	A	R	N
I	F	A	T	H	E	R	O	E	S	M	A	Y
W	P	S	N	E	W	O	J	T	J	M	W	A
F	N	G	W	R	N	T	Y	S	X	A	G	C
H	W	S	P	X	D	H	H	I	M	T	D	K
U	N	C	L	E	U	E	Y	S	Y	E	H	F
S	U	N	T	P	A	R	E	N	T	S	I	O
B	L	C	L	A	S	S	M	A	T	E	S	P
A	Z	X	C	V	B	N	L	K	J	H	G	F
N	G	R	A	N	D	P	A	R	E	N	T	S
D	Q	W	E	R	T	U	I	O	P	A	S	D

3 Use the words to write sentences about your family.

aunt	grandfather
brother	grandmother
classmates	mother
cousin	sister
father	uncle

1. _____ *My sister Carol is twelve.* _____

2. _____

3. _____

4. _____

5. _____

6. _____

GRAMMAR *have*

1 Complete the chart.

John's FAMILY	
Affirmative	**Negative**
1. I ___*have*___ three brothers.	I _____ any sisters.
2. My cousin Janet _____ two sisters.	My cousin Janet _____ any brothers.
3. My grandparents _____ six children.	They _____ a small family.
4. My brother Jack _____ a cat named Max.	He _____ a pet snake.
5. My mother and father _____ big family parties.	They _____ small family parties.

2 Circle the correct form of *have*.

1. John **has / have** a cousin named Janet.

2. John and his brothers **don't have / don't has** any sisters.

3. John's brother Jack **don't has / doesn't have** a pet snake.

4. John **has / have** lots of aunts and uncles.

3 Answer the questions.

1. Does John have a baby sister?

    No, John doesn't have a baby sister.

2. Do John and Jack have a big family?

    _____

3. Do John's parents have family parties?

    _____

4. Does John's brother Jack have a cat?

    _____

5. Does John's cousin Janet have any brothers?

    _____

4 Write sentences about you. Use *have* or *don't have*.

1. Cell phone?

    I don't have a cell phone.

2. Comic books?

    _____

3. Game console?

    _____

4. Soccer ball?

    _____

5. Inline skates?

    _____

6. Guitar?

    _____

7. Big family?

    _____

1 Match the pictures with the correct descriptions. Write a sentence for each.

 1   Eduardo    2   Tammy    3   Jessie    4   Erica

_____   *Tammy has short, light*   _____   _____

_____   *wavy hair.*   _____   _____

a. short, light wavy hair   b. long, dark straight hair

c. short, dark curly hair   d. long, dark curly hair

2 Draw two people in the boxes. Give them names. Then write a sentence describing each one.

Name: _____

_____

_____

Name: _____

_____

_____

3 Write five sentences describing a good friend or someone in your family.

1. _____ *My friend Leah is very funny and really intelligent.* _____

2. _____

3. _____

4. _____

5. _____

6. _____

GRAMMAR Comparative adjectives

Cathy   Brad   Jake

1 Circle the correct answers.

1. Cathy is **younger** / more younger than Brad and Jake.

2. Cathy is **shorter** / **more short** than Brad and Jake.

3. Cathy's hair is **curly** / **curlier** than Jake's hair.

4. Brad is **taller** / **more tall** than Cathy and Jake.

5. Jake is **older** / **more old** than Cathy.

6. Brad's hair is **darker** / **more dark** than Cathy's hair.

2 Write four sentences about Cathy, Brad, and Jake. Use comparative adjectives and *than*.

1. *Jake's hair is straighter than Cathy's hair.*

2. _____

3. _____

4. _____

5. _____

3 Complete the paragraph with comparative adjectives and *than*.

Jackie and her friend Stella are very different. Jackie is
1 _____*taller than*_____ (tall) Stella, and her hair
is 2 _____ (dark) Stella's hair.
Stella is 3 _____ (short) Jackie,
and her hair is 4 _____ (wavy)
Jackie's hair. Stella thinks she is 5 _____
(funny) Jackie, but they are both very funny!

4 Complete the chart with the correct pronouns.

Possessive adjectives	Possessive pronouns
my	*mine*
_____	yours
his	_____
_____	hers
our	_____
their	_____

5 Correct the possessive adjectives and possessive pronouns.

   My   *yours*
1. ~~Mine~~ hair is curlier than ~~you~~.

2. You hair is longer than my.

3. His hair is wavier than their.

4. Our sister is older than yours sister.

5. Hers brother's eyes are bluer than your.

6. He is more intelligent than hers brother.

1 Match the questions with the answers.

1. Hi, Paul. How are you?   a. Sure. I'm not busy.

2. Sorry, can I call you back?   b. It's 980-555-2535.

3. Can you hold on a minute?   c. I'm fine. How are you?

4. Do you have Jordan's email?   d. OK. I'll wait.

5. What's Jordan's phone number?   e. It's jb5@schoolemail.com.

2 Put the sentences in order to make a conversation.

_____	**Andrew:**	I'm good, thanks. Hey, do you have John's phone number and email?
_____	**Amy:**	Hold on a minute. Yes, here they are. His phone number is 825-555-9944. His email is johnw@online.com.
_____	**Amy:**	Hi, Andrew. How are you?
_____	**Andrew:**	Hi, Amy. It's Andrew.
1	**Amy:**	Hello?
_____	**Amy:**	I'll have to ask my parents. Can I call you back?
_____	**Andrew:**	Sure. Call back soon, and we can make plans.
_____	**Andrew:**	Thanks. I want to ask John to go to the movies tomorrow. Can you come, too?

READING TO WRITE

1 Circle the intensifiers.

1. David has blue eyes and is very tall and really handsome.

2. Their house is not very big, but it's really nice.

3. His father is very handsome, but he isn't very tall.

4. I love to read, but I'm not really interested in comic books.

2 Complete the word web with information about Justin Timberlake.

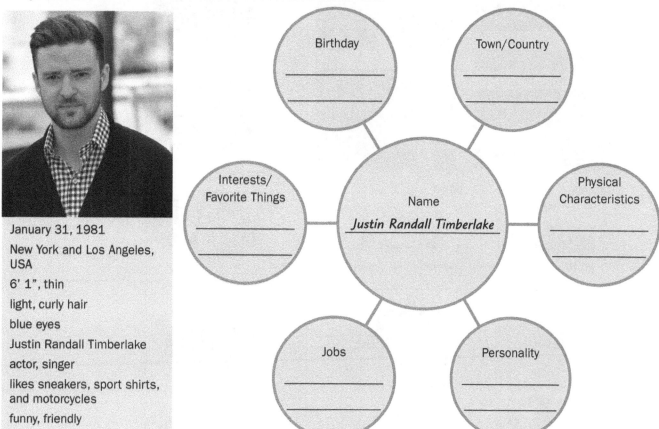

January 31, 1981

New York and Los Angeles, USA

6' 1", thin

light, curly hair

blue eyes

Justin Randall Timberlake

actor, singer

likes sneakers, sport shirts, and motorcycles

funny, friendly

3 Write four sentences about Justin Timberlake. Use intensifiers.

1. _____ *Justin has very blue eyes.* _____

2. _____

3. _____

4. _____

5. _____

4 *It's My* **LIFE**

1 Complete the crossword.

```
          1
2     ³b  e  d     4
5
              6
7
         8
```

across

3. go to
   bed

4. get

5. do some

6. start

7. do my

8. get

down

1. have

2. brush my

3. have

6. take a

2 Write the phrases from Exercise 1 in the order of your daily routine.

	have lunch
	have dinner
	go to bed

3 Choose four phrases from Exercise 2. Write sentences with your own information.

1. _____*I get up at 7:00 a.m.*_____
2. _____
3. _____
4. _____
5. _____

GRAMMAR Simple present statements

1 Circle the correct words.

1. You **go** / **goes** to school at 8:00 a.m.

2. He **finish** / **finishes** soccer at 6:00 p.m.

3. I **study** / **studies** very hard.

4. She **teach** / **teaches** Spanish.

5. They **play** / **plays** soccer after school.

6. We **do** / **does** our homework after school.

7. She **have** / **has** a big smile.

2 Write sentences from Exercise 1 and make them negative.

1. _You don't go to school at 8:00 a.m._

2. _____

3. _____

4. _____

5. _____

6. _____

7. _____

3 Complete the sentences.

1. I _____ before the test.

2. We _____ lunch at noon.

3. My brother _____ soccer on the beach.

4. She _____ her homework every day.

5. You _____ at 6:30 a.m. every morning.

6. I _____ to school on the weekends.

4 Complete the text with the correct forms of the verbs.

Elias and Paul are eleven. They ¹_____go_____ (go) to a secondary school in Germany. They ²_____ (not wear) a uniform. They ³_____ (study) English, Latin, and 13 other subjects. They ⁴_____ (start) school at 7:30 a.m. and ⁵_____ (finish) classes at 1:30 p.m. Elias and Paul ⁶_____ (not have) lunch at school. Elias ⁷_____ (eat) at Paul's house with Paul's family. Elias's parents ⁸_____ (work) all day. After lunch, Paul and Elias ⁹_____ (play) sports. Sometimes Paul ¹⁰_____ (play) games while Elias ¹¹_____ (do) his chores. Then they both ¹²_____ (do) their homework.

5 Correct the sentences. One sentence is correct.

plays
1. Eric ~~play~~ baseball on weekends.

2. We goes to a restaurant on Saturdays.

3. Cati do her homework in bed.

4. My cousins visits us for the holidays.

5. I get up early on Saturdays.

6. I shops for clothes with my parents.

7. My best friend watch football on TV.

VOCABULARY After-school activities

1 Put the letters in order to make after-school activities.

1. SUCIM
   music

2. NETSIN
   _____

3. SHECS
   _____

4. GWINMISM
   _____

5. RAT SECSALS
   _____

6. ATAKER
   _____

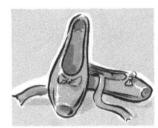 

7. DENAC SEASLSC
   _____

8. RAMAD
   _____

2 Write the after-school activities from Exercise 1 in the correct columns.

Do	Go	Play	Take
		music	

3 Circle the activity that doesn't belong.

1. soccer
2. tennis
3. drama
4. swimming
5. karate

4 Write the activities in the correct columns.

~~art~~	drama	music	swimming
dance	karate	soccer	tennis

Arts	Sports
art	

GRAMMAR Simple present questions

1 Complete the chart with your own information. Write ✗ or ✓.

	Robert	Clara	_____
does karate	✗	✓	
goes swimming	✓	✓	
plays tennis	✗	✓	
takes dance classes	✗	✗	
takes art classes	✓	✗	
does drama	✓	✓	
plays music	✓	✗	

2 Write short answers to the questions. Use the information from the chart in Exercise 1.

1. Does Clara do karate?

   _____ *Yes, she does.* _____

2. Do Robert and Clara go swimming?

   _____

3. Does Robert play tennis?

   _____

4. Do Robert and Clara take dance classes?

   _____

5. Does Clara take art classes?

   _____

6. Do you do karate?

   _____

7. Do you play music?

   _____

3 Complete the sentences with the correct Wh- word.

1. ___*What*___ music do you and your friends like? We like hip-hop music.

2. _____ do you go after school? We go to the park.

3. _____ do they go to the movies? They go on Saturday night.

4. _____ do you go to the movies with? I go with my best friend, Jessie.

5. _____ does your friend play the violin? She plays the violin because she likes classical music.

4 Complete the questions.

1. A: _____ *Do you eat* _____ (you / eat) a lot of vegetables?

   B: Yes, I do.

2. A: _____ (your brother / play) the guitar?

   B: No, he doesn't.

3. A: _____ (Elias and Paul / finish) school at 1:30?

   B: Yes, they do.

4. A: _____ (you / like) comics, Paula?

   B: No, I don't.

5. A: _____ (you all / play) tennis at school?

   B: No, we don't.

5 Answer the questions with your own information. Use complete sentences.

1. Do you play basketball?

   _____ *Yes, I do. / No, I don't.* _____

2. Where do you go to school?

   _____

3. Do you play in the school band?

   _____

4. When do you go to bed?

   _____

5. What kind of music do you like?

   _____

Adverbs of frequency

Correct the adverbs of frequency. One sentence is correct.

   usually
1. I get up ~~usually~~ early in the morning.

2. I play often tennis on the weekend.

3. I never am late to class.

4. I always am happy on Friday night.

5. I sometimes have lunch with my friend.

6. I go to bed late on the weekend usually.

1 **Put the words in the correct order to make phrases for asking for information.**

1. welcome / You're / .

   <u>You're welcome.</u>

2. close / does / time / What / the library / ?

   _____

3. days / the library / is / What / open / ?

   _____

4. a library card / you / Do / have / ?

   _____

5. can / How / you / I / help / ?

   _____

6. like / I'd / please / some information, / .

   _____

7. much / is / it / How / ?

   _____

2 **Complete the conversation with phrases from Exercise 1.**

Robin: Welcome to the Fairview Public Library! My name's Robin.
¹ <u>How can I help you?</u>

Dawn: Hi, Robin. ² _____ Do you have any books about Idina Menzel?

Robin: Yes, we do. They're in the biographies section.

Dawn: Great!

Robin: ³ _____

Dawn: No, I don't. ⁴ _____

Robin: The card is free, but there are late fees. It's $1 a day for DVDs and 25¢ a day for books.

Dawn: OK. ⁵ _____

Robin: It's open Monday through Saturday.

Dawn: ⁶ _____

Robin: It closes at 7:00.

Dawn: That's good. OK, I'll get a library card.

Robin: OK. Please write your name and address on this form. . . . Great! Here's your card.

Dawn: Perfect, thanks!

Robin: ⁷ _____ Have a nice day!

Dawn: Thanks, you too!

READING TO WRITE

1 Complete Blake's letter with *and*, *or*, or *but*.

Hi Blake,

My question is: What is your routine before the soccer world championships?
Marisol!
P. S. Good luck!

---

i Marisol,

Monday through Friday, I always get up at 6:00,
¹___*and*___ I eat a big breakfast.

After dinner, around 8:00, I do my homework.
don't have a lot of free time, ²_____
ometimes I watch TV ³_____ chat online
ith my friends.

---

tart school at 8:30 ⁴_____ finish at 3:00.

I go to bed at 10:30.

---

eat dinner at 7:15.

At 3:30 I run ⁵_____ kick the soccer ball for
three hours, so I get home at around 7:00.

---

n the weekends, I play soccer for four
_____ five hours, but on Saturday evening,
usually go to the movies or hang out with
y friends.

ake

2 Put the pieces of Blake's letter to Marisol in the correct order.

Hi Marisol,

Monday through Friday, I always get up at 6:00
_____ I eat a big breakfast.

_____

_____

_____

_____

_____

_____

_____

_____

_____

_____

_____

_____

On weekends, I play soccer for four
_____ five hours, but on Saturday
evening, I usually go to the movies or hang out
with my friends.

Blake

1 Look at the pictures of Eleanor's family and friends. Circle the correct words in the questions and write the answers.

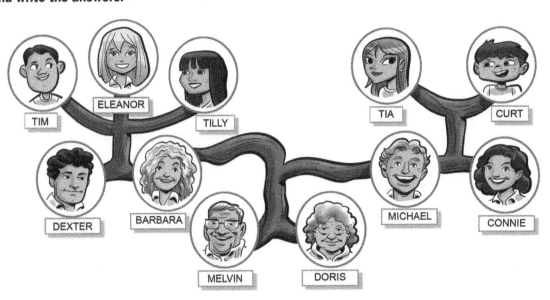

1. **Does** / **Do** Michael **have** / **has** white hair?

   _____No, he doesn't._____

2. **Do** / **Does** Connie and Michael **have** / **has** wavy hair?

   _____

3. **Do** / **Does** Curt **have** / **has** a sister?

   _____

4. **Do** / **Does** Eleanor **have** / **has** a brother?

   _____

5. **Do** / **Does** Tim and Tilly **have** / **has** cousins?

   _____

2 Complete Eleanor's sentences.

curly	handsome	pretty
dark	intelligent	wavy
funny	light	young

1. My parents, Barbara and Dexter, have _____ hair.

2. My mom, Barbara, and I have _____ hair.

3. Aunt Connie and Uncle Michael have _____ hair.

4. My cousin, Tia, is good-looking. Tia is _____.

5. Uncle Michael is good-looking, too. Uncle Michael is _____.

6. My brother, Tim, knows a lot of things. He is _____.

7. My cousin, Curt, is only seven. He is _____.

3 Complete Timmy's daily routine. Use the words in the box.

always	goes	takes
arrives	never	usually
eats	sometimes	wakes

Every morning, Timmy [1]_____ up at 6:30.
He [2]_____ a shower every day at 7:00. He
[3]_____ does this at the same time. Most days,
he [4]_____ breakfast. After breakfast, Timmy
[5]_____ to school. He [6]_____
walks to school, but other times he takes the bus. He
[7]_____ at school each morning at 8:00. He
is [8]_____ late. He [9]_____ has
Reading first, but on Fridays, he has Spanish first.

4 Complete the sentences.

Cindy   Jill   Cheryl

1. Jill is _____ than Cindy.

2. Cindy is _____ Cheryl and Jill.

3. Cheryl's hair is _____ Cindy's hair.

4. Jill's hair is _____ Cheryl's hair.

5 Look at the pictures in Exercise 5. Complete the sentences.

1. Cindy _____ dance classes after school.

2. Jill _____ soccer on weekends.

3. Cheryl always _____ her homework.

4. Cheryl _____ very hard.

6 Complete the sentences with *always, usually, sometimes,* or *never.*

Jake	Michael	Kyle
Plays tennis every day from 3:00–5:00 p.m.	Plays tennis most Mondays and Wednesdays from 4:00–6:00 p.m. and most weekends	Plays tennis once in a while on Sundays

1. Michael _____ plays tennis on Tuesdays.

2. Jake _____ plays tennis from 3:00 to 5:00 p.m.

3. Kyle _____ plays tennis on Sundays.

4. Michael _____ plays tennis on the weekends.

5. Jake _____ plays tennis at 6:00 p.m.

7 Complete the phone conversation with the expressions. There is one extra expression.

call you back	How are you	Sure
Hi	It's	Talk to you soon
Hold on	jharris3@ schoolemail.com	212-555-8927

Andrea: Hello?

Paul: Hi. ¹_____ Paul.

Andrea: ²_____, Paul.

Paul: ³_____?

Andrea: Good, thanks.

Paul: Hey, do you have Jason's cell phone number?

Andrea: Um, yes. ⁴_____ a minute. Okay, it's ⁵_____.

Paul: I want him to come over and play video games. Can you come over, too?

Andrea: When?

Paul: I don't know yet. Can I ⁶_____?

Andrea: ⁷_____.

Paul: Good. ⁸_____.

8 You want to take art classes. You call the Waterford Art Center. Look at the schedule and complete the questions.

Name of class	Day / Time	Room number	Price per class
Drawing Comics	Mon. and Wed. / 3:30 p.m.	Room 3	$5.00
Painting	Tues. and Thurs. / 5:00 p.m.	Room 6	$7.00
Computer Graphics	Sat. / 10:00 a.m.	Room 4	$5.00

1. What _____*are the names of the classes?*_____

   The names of the classes are Drawing Comics, Painting, and Computer Graphics.

2. When_____

   That class is on Monday and Wednesday at 3:30.

3. What_____

   It starts at 5:00 p.m.

4. Where_____

   That class is in Room 4.

5. How_____

   It costs $7.

5 School Days

1 Put the letters in the correct order to make words. Then write the name of each place under its picture.

DGAYRUPLNO   _____

CSENICE BLA   _____

BRLYARI   _____

YMG   _____

FTACEIRAE   _____

RTA OORM   _____

UDAMORTIUI   _____

SMOSOLACR   _____

NMIA FFICOE   _____

PCUMRTEO ABL   _____

1 _____

2 _____

3 _____

4 _____

5 _____

6 _____

7 _____

8 _____

9 _____

10 _____

2 Write each place from Exercise 1 in the correct column.

Places to study in school	Other places at school
	main office

3 Write sentences to tell what you do at the other places at school from Exercise 2.

1. *I go to the main office when I have questions about school.*

2. _____

_____

3. _____

_____

4. _____

_____

5. _____

_____

1 Complete the chart.

Affirmative	Negative
1. We / They / You _____*can*_____ sing well.	2. We / They / You _____ sing well.
Questions	**Answers**
3. _____ I / he / she / it sing well?	4. Yes, I / he / she / it _____ sing well.
	5. No, I / he / she / it _____ sing well.

2 Look at the pictures. Answer the questions using *can* and *can't*.

1. Can Vicky play the guitar?

   No, she can't.

2. Can Cathy do judo?

   _____

3. Can Alex sing?

   _____

4. Can Erin play tennis?

   _____

5. Can Mia play basketball?

   _____

6. Can Steven play the guitar?

   _____

3 Put the words in the correct order to ask questions. Then answer the questions with your own information.

1. talk / in / your / to / Can / your / friends / class / ?

   Can you talk to your friends in class?

   No, I can't. / Yes, I can.

2. you / Can / play / guitar / the / ?

   _____

   _____

3. you / speak / Can / Chinese / ?

   _____

   _____

4. ride / you / Can / horse / a / ?

   _____

   _____

5. kung fu / your / Can / do / mother / ?

   _____

   _____

6. can / songs / you / What / sing / ?

   _____

   _____

4 Complete the sentences with *can* or *can't*.

1. I just got new glasses. Now I _____*can*_____ see the board.

2. Jason has a strong voice. He _____ sing very well.

3. Jessie has to babysit this weekend. She

   _____ come to my party on Saturday.

4. My legs aren't very strong. I _____ run very fast.

5. Terry is only 11. She _____ drive yet.

School subjects

1 Find seven more school subjects.

✓civics	ICT
English	math
geography	PE
history	science

Q	W	E	R	T	Y	G	U	I
S	C	T	R	M	A	E	W	D
B	I	H	I	S	T	O	R	Y
F	V	U	L	B	O	G	K	S
A	I	F	P	E	C	R	O	E
I	C	T	N	C	M	A	T	H
F	S	G	W	V	N	P	Y	S
E	N	G	L	I	S	H	E	B
U	N	C	L	C	U	Y	Y	S
C	S	C	I	E	N	C	E	N

2 Write each word from Exercise 1 next to the correct picture.

1. _____civics_____

2. _____

3. _____

4. _____

5. _____

6. _____

7. _____

8. _____

3 In which classes would you hear these questions? Write the school subjects.

1. "Where is Italy on a map?" ___geography___

2. "What's 9 × 12?" _____

3. "How big is the sun?" _____

4. "Who was the first president of the United States of America?" _____

5. "What does *swim* mean?" _____

6. "How fast can you run?" _____

4 Correct the incorrect sentences. Write *correct* if no changes are needed.

1. Our class studies history in the cafeteria.

   Our class studies history in the classroom.

2. We have PE in the auditorium.

   _____

3. *ICT* means "Information Communication Technology."

   _____

4. *PE* means "Physical Exercise."

   _____

5. We have ICT in the science lab.

   _____

6. We study maps in math class.

   _____

5 Complete the sentences with your own information.

1. In PE ___I can run faster than my classmates___

2. In history we study _____.

3. In math class I _____.

4. I go to the library _____.

5. In science class we _____.

6. _____ is my favorite subject because _____.

7. _____ is my least favorite subject because _____.

8. In English class we can _____

GRAMMAR Object pronouns; verb + -*ing* form (gerund) for opinions

1 Underline the subject pronouns. Circle the object pronouns.

1. <u>I</u> am in an art class. <u>I</u> really like (it).

2. My brother gives music lessons to my friends and me. He gives them to us for free.

3. Miss Grant gives books to Sophie, but she always reads them first.

4. Does Dina study French?
   Yes, she's very good at it.

5. Do Sherrell and Ivy take karate lessons?
   Yes, they take them on weekends.

6. Sonya usually kicks the ball to Wendy, but she never kicks it to me.

2 Match the questions with the correct answers.

1. Do you like football?
2. Do you like computer classes?
3. Do you like Bill?
4. Does Tom like you?
5. Does your teacher like you and your classmates?

a. Yes, I like them.
b. Yes, she likes us.
c. Yes, I like it.
d. Yes, I like him.
e. No, he doesn't like me.

3 Complete the sentences with subject and object pronouns.

1. My favorite subject in school is PE.
   _____*I*_____ really like _____*it*_____.

2. Bob really doesn't like civics and geography.
   _____ really doesn't like
   _____.

3. Mary and Inez love Harry Styles. _____ love _____.

4. Jim hates pop music. _____ hates
   _____.

5. Jennifer and I hate doing homework.
   _____ hate _____.

4 Circle the correct words.

1. I like **play / playing** the guitar. I'm really good at **play / playing / it**.

2. He can **speak / speaking** Japanese really well! He loves **studies it / studying it**.

3. We **do / doing** homework after dinner. We like **do / doing** it together.

4. She doesn't **like / mind** her ICT class because she's good at **work / working / it** on computers.

5. Hector hates **dance / dancing** when his friends watch him. He **dances / dancing** when he is at home.

5 Use the -*ing* form of the verbs to write sentences that express opinion.

Verbs	Opinions
dance	love
~~do~~	like
eat	don't mind
play	don't like
sing	hate
study	
watch	

1. _____ *I love doing karate.* _____

2. _____

3. _____

4. _____

5. _____

6. _____

7. _____

1 **Put the words in the correct order to make sentences to complete the conversation.**

A: go / May / library, / please / I / to / the / ?

_____*May I go to the library, please?*_____

B: for / No. / time / is / It / geography / .

_____

A: But / left / my / geography / in the library /
book / I / .

_____

B: can / share / You / a / with / book / Diane / .

_____

A: get / May / I / it / lunch / during / ?

_____

B: No / Sure. / problem / .

_____

2 **Complete the sentences.**

But	can	~~may~~	sorry	Sure	Thanks

Justin: Mr. Mitchell, [1]_____*may*_____ I stay after class for help with math today?

Mr. Mitchell: I'm [2]_____, Justin, but I have to go somewhere after school today.

Justin: [3]_____ we have a math test tomorrow.

Mr. Mitchell: Haley, [4]_____ you help Justin after school with math?

Haley: [5]_____, no problem, Mr. Mitchell.

Mr. Mitchell: [6]_____, Haley.

READING TO WRITE

1 Put the steps for an email request in order.

_____ Say thank you.

_____ Ask for permission to do something.

___1___ Introduce yourself.

_____ State the problem.

2 Write the email in the correct order. Then label the parts of the email with the words and phrases.

```
○○○
📄 📁 ◁ 📎 🗑
   To  [                                                    ]
 From  [ lmichaels@clstudent.cup.org                        ]
Subject[                                                    ]

   Dear Mr. Sanchez,
```

Ask for permission.	Closing	Greeting	Introduce yourself.
Say thank you.	State the problem.	Subject line	

Dear Mr. Sanchez, _____Greeting_____

sanchezt@clmiddleschool.cup.org

I'm a student in your math class. _____

Thank you for considering this. _____

May I stay after school a couple of days for extra help? _____

If you can help me, please let me know what days you can stay.

I try to do my homework, but many times I don't understand it. _____

Math is very hard for me. _____

Best regards, _____

Lee _____

Help with homework _____

I'm Lee Michaels. _____

6 Time to Eat

VOCABULARY Food

1 Put the letters in the correct order to make food words. Then write the name of each food under its picture.

1. ANANASB ___bananas___

2. EANBS _____

3. EESEHC _____

4. DEBAR _____

5. ESOMATOT _____

6. FEBE _____

7. NEKCICH _____

8. RORTACS _____

9. TAPTESOO _____

a   _carrots_   b _____

c _____   d _____

e _____   f _____

g _____   h _____

i _____

2 Circle the correct answers.

1. Which one is a vegetable?

   a. chicken   b. carrots   c. eggs

2. Which one is a fruit?

   a. beans   b. oranges   c. milk

3. Which one do people often eat for breakfast?

   a. beef   b. carrots   c. eggs

4. Which is a food that vegetarians do NOT eat?

   a. fruits   b. beef   c. vegetables

3 Complete the sentences.

animals	apples	juice	plants

1. Oranges, bananas, and _____ are fruits.

2. Cheese, eggs, and beef come from _____.

3. Oranges, potatoes, and tomatoes come from _____.

4. Milk, water, and _____ are things to drink.

4 Answer the questions with complete sentences.

1. What are five foods you like to eat?

I like to eat beef, cheese, potatoes, tomatoes,

and oranges.

2. What is your favorite food?

_____

3. How often do you eat your favorite food?

_____

4. What are three things you like to drink?

_____

_____

5. What is your favorite drink?

_____

6. How often do you drink your favorite drink?

_____

GRAMMAR a / an; some and any with countable and uncountable nouns

1 Write each word in the correct column.

apple	burger	corn	meat
banana	~~carrot~~	egg	tomato
bread	cheese	juice	rice

Countable nouns	Uncountable nouns
carrot	

2 Complete the text with *a/an*, *some*, or *any*.

Jeremy plays football. He loves meat, but he doesn't eat a lot of it, and he doesn't eat ¹_____ *any* _____ takeout food.

Here's what he usually eats:

Breakfast: ²_____ fruit, ³_____ big plate of eggs, ⁴_____ bread, and ⁵_____ milk.

Snack after training: ⁶_____ sports drink and ⁷_____ bananas. He doesn't eat ⁸_____ potato chips.

Lunch: ⁹_____ pizza, ¹⁰_____ apple, and ¹¹_____ water.

Dinner: ¹²_____ fish, a lot of potatoes and ¹³_____ vegetables.

3 Write sentences using *a/an*, *some*, or *any* for three countable and three uncountable nouns in Exercise 1.

1. ___*I eat some carrots for lunch every day.*___ OR
   ___*I eat a carrot for lunch every day.*___ OR
   ___*I don't eat any carrots.*___
2. _____
3. _____
4. _____
5. _____
6. _____
7. _____

1 Circle 12 more food words.

sandwichtacossaladsushipastacakeicecreamburgercerealyogurtcrackersnutssoup

2 Write the names of the meals on the timeline.

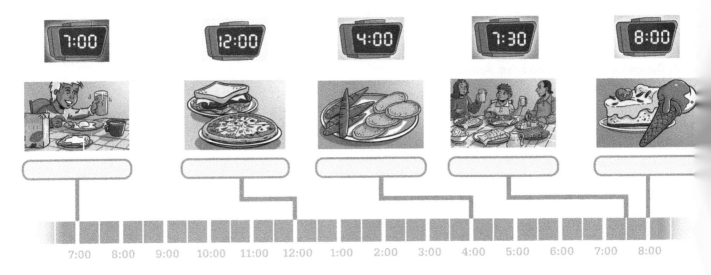

7:00 8:00 9:00 10:00 11:00 12:00 1:00 2:00 3:00 4:00 5:00 6:00 7:00 8:00

3 What do you eat at meals? Write the food words in the word web. Add your own ideas. Some words can go in more than one circle.

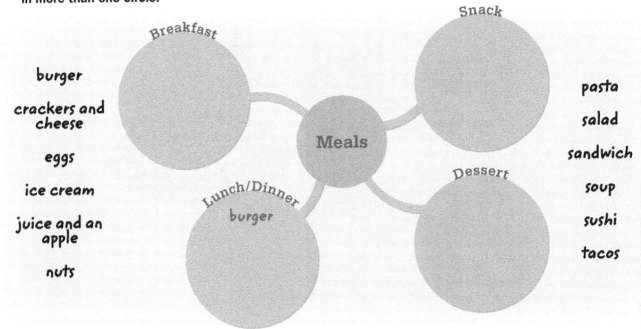

burger

crackers and cheese

eggs

ice cream

juice and an apple

nuts

Breakfast

Snack

Meals

Lunch/Dinner
burger

Dessert

pasta

salad

sandwich

soup

sushi

tacos

GRAMMAR *there is/are* with *much, many,* and *a lot of*

1 Circle the correct words.

1. *There is a +* ⟨**singular**⟩ */ **plural*** countable noun.
2. *There is some +* **countable / uncountable** noun.
3. *There are some +* **singular / plural** countable noun.
4. *There isn't* **some / any** + noun.
5. *There aren't* **some / any** + noun.

2 Correct the sentences.

         is some
1. There ~~are any~~ cheese in the refrigerator.

2. Are there some milk?

3. There isn't an oranges.

4. There are any bananas?

5. Are there some rice?

6. There aren't a pasta.

3 Circle the correct answers.

1. How **many / much** bananas are there?

2. How **much / many** juice is there?

3. There is **a lot of / many** milk on the table.

4. There is **much / a lot** of food on my plate.

5. There are **much / many** oranges in the basket.

6. There is **many / a lot** of water in the pot.

4 Complete the conversation.

A: Do you want a snack?

B: Sure! ¹_____ cake left from yesterday?

A: No, there ²_____ cake, but there ³_____ a lot of cheese.

B: Cheese and crackers sound good. ⁴_____ there ⁵_____ crackers?

A: Oh, no. No crackers, but ⁶_____ bread and a tomato. We could make cheese and tomato sandwiches.

B: Sounds good!

5 Look in the fridge. Answer the questions. Use *some, a lot of, much, an,* and *any*.

1. How much milk is there?

        There isn't much milk.
_____

2. How many apples are there?

_____

3. How much bread is there?

_____

4. How much juice is there?

_____

5. How many carrots are there?

_____

6. How much cheese is there?

_____

7. How much cake is there?

_____

1 **Put the words in the correct order to make questions. Then match the questions with the correct answers.**

1. can / get / you / What / I / ?

_____*What can I get you?*_____

2. Can / get / you / else / anything / I / ?

_____

3. you / of soup / do / want / What / kind / ?

_____

4. to drink / Can / you / get / something / I / ?

_____

a. Tomato soup. Thank you.

b. Yes. I'd like some orange juice, please.

c. I'd also like some soup.

d. Can I have a fish sandwich?

2 **Look at the menu. Write sentences or questions for ordering lunch at this café.**

MENU

DRINKS
milk

juice
* changes *
by the
day

tea

coffee

water

DESSERTS
chocolate cake

orange ice cream

SANDWICHES, ETC.
fish tacos

chicken and cheese
sandwich

fish sandwich

lettuce and tomato
sandwich

SOUP
tomato

potato

chicken rice

chili

* Ask about our
soup of the day. *

1. Ask a question about the soup of the day.

_____*What is the soup of the day?*_____

2. Order a sandwich. Use *I'd like.*

_____

3. Ask a question about juice. Use *kinds of.*

_____

4. Order soup. Use *Can I have.*

_____

5. Ask a question about the chili. Use *have meat.*

_____

6. Order a sandwich. Make your own kind.

_____

1 Complete the invitation with the correct question words.

Who

What

When

Where

Invitation
Elena's Birthday Party

The Rainbow Café
25 Prospect Road • Mason, Ohio

Elena's soccer teammates

Saturday, April 12 • Noon

2 Circle four more time connectors.

> Before dinner, I do my homework. While I eat dinner, I talk to my family about my day.
> After dinner, I have dessert. Then I watch soccer on TV before I go to bed.

3 Put the events in order. Then write a paragraph about a basketball game. Use time connectors.

_____ Celebrate with my teammates

_____ Make 10 points

___*1*___ Put on my basketball clothes

_____ Walk home

_____ Walk to the game

_____ Win the game

Before I walk to the game, I put on my basketball clothes.

_____

_____

_____

_____

_____

1 Put the words in the correct columns.

art room	fish	math
cafeteria	history	meat
cheese	ICT	sandwich
civics	library	science lab
English	main office	sushi

School places	School subjects	Foods

2 Write four uncountable foods from Exercise 1.

1. _____

2. _____

3. _____

4. _____

3 Complete the paragraph with foods you eat.

> I sometimes have ¹_____ for breakfast. I
> usually have ²_____ for lunch. I often drink
> ³_____ with my lunch. I don't like
> ⁴_____ so I never have it for a snack. I usually
> have ⁵_____ or ⁶_____ for a
> snack. For dinner, I often have ⁷_____ with
> ⁸_____. And for dessert I have
> ⁹_____.

4 Complete the sentences with Is there, are there, there is, or there are. Then match the questions with the answers.

1. _____ a. _____
   any milk in the fridge?   a lot of sushi.
   _____

2. _____ b. Yes, there is.
   any potatoes in the kitchen?
   _____

3. How much sushi   c. _____
   _____?   three carrots.
   _____

4. How many carrots   d. Yes, there are.
   _____?
   _____

5 Complete the conversation.

a lot of
any
Are there
How many
many
much
there are
there is

Alex: Let's make a salad.

Gina: Good idea! ¹_____ any
vegetables?

Alex: Yes, ²_____. We have
carrots.

Gina: ³_____ tomatoes are
there?

Alex: There aren't ⁴_____ –
just two. But they're very big.

Gina: How ⁵_____
cheese is there?

Alex: There's ⁶_____
cheese.

Gina: Is there ⁷_____ soup
to go with our salad?

Alex: Yes, ⁸_____ a lot
of potato soup.

6 Circle the correct words.

1. Josh: **Can / Do** you like **playing / doing** kung fu?

   Nick: Yes, I love **them / it**.

2. Jake: What sports **can / do** you and **your / you** brother like?

   Howard: **Us / We** like playing basketball, but **us / we** don't play that well.

3. Sally: **We / Us** need help with **our / us** homework.

   Bettina: I'm sure **me / my** older sister **may / can** help.

4. Jack: **Can / Do** you give **we / us** a ride to the park to go skateboarding?

   Brooke: Yes, sure. **I / Me** can take **us / you**.

5. Terry: **You / We** can play baseball better than **me / it**.

   Jackson: Thanks, Terry. **I / You** are nice to say that!

7 Put the words in the correct order to ask for and give permission.

1. I / go / the / main office / to / Can / ?

   _____

2. You / go / may / class / during / not / .

   _____

3. I / to / have / give / an / them / important / letter / .

   _____

4. you / go / on your way / class / to / next / your / Can / ?

   _____

5. no / problem / Sure, /.

   _____

8 Match the answers to the questions.

a. Yes, that's right, thank you.

b. A steak salad.

c. I'd like a salad, please.

d. Just water, please.

e. Oh yes, some carrot soup, too.

A: What can I get you?

B: ¹ _____

A: What kind of salad do you want?

B: ² _____

A: Anything else?

B: ³ _____

A: Anything to drink?

B: ⁴ _____

A: OK. That's a steak salad, carrot soup, and water.

B: ⁵ _____

7 Animal World

1 Circle 17 more animals.

spider sheep polarbearbirdzebragiraffeelephantmonkeytigerfishhorsepiggorillasharkdogcatcowfrog

2 Circle the correct answers.

1. Which animal DOESN'T live in water?

   a. fish   b. frog   c. giraffe

2. Which animal DOESN'T live on a farm?

   a. cow   b. monkey   c. horse

3. Which animal DOESN'T eat plants?

   a. lion   b. cow   c. sheep

4. Which animal DOESN'T eat meat?

   a. dog   b. tiger   c. cow

3 Choose five animals from Exercise 1. Write a sentence about each animal. Use words from the box.

eat bugs	eat plants	fly
live in Africa	swim	

1. _____ *Polar bears can't fly.* _____

2. _____

3. _____

4. _____

5. _____

6. _____

4 Complete the sentences with your own ideas.

1. My favorite water animal is the _____*frog*_____
   because _____*it can jump high*_____.

2. My favorite farm animal is the _____
   because _____.

3. I love _____ because
   _____.

4. I don't like _____ because
   _____.

5. I want to learn more about _____
   because _____.

1 Look at Sam's photos from the zoo. Correct the sentences with the present continuous of the verbs. Use contractions.

eat	play	stand
look	~~sleep~~	swim

1. The lions are fighting.

_____The lions aren't fighting. They're sleeping._____

2. The baby gorilla is eating its lunch in the tree.

_____

_____

3. I'm looking at a frog.

_____

_____

4. The monkeys are drinking.

_____

_____

5. The polar bears are sleeping.

_____

_____

6. He's sitting next to an elephant.

_____

_____

2 Complete the conversation with the present continuous form of the verbs. Use contractions.

Kari: Are these your photos from Safari Park?

Rose: Yes. Look. Here are the tigers.
They [1]_____'re watching_____ (watch) us, but
they [2]_____ (not do)
anything. In this photo, the baby tigers
[3]_____ (fight)! Aren't
they cute?

Kari: [4]_____ (the monkey
hide)?

Rose: No, he [5]_____ (play)!

Kari: Oh, right!

Rose: And here, I [6]_____
(look) at a snake.

Kari: Oooh! What [7]_____
(your mom do)?

Rose: She [8]_____ (run) away!

3 Write questions in the present continuous. Answer the questions for you. Use contractions.

1. What / you / study / in science?

_____What are you studying in science?_____

_____I'm studying the weather._____

2. What / after-school activities / you / do?

_____

_____

3. What / you / do / in gym class?

_____

_____

4. What / you / read / in English?

_____

_____

VOCABULARY Action verbs

1 Find six more action verbs.

S	W	I	N	G	I	N	G	H
K	Z	L	H	C	D	B	U	I
S	W	I	M	M	I	N	G	D
R	Y	H	Q	A	T	U	D	I
Z	H	G	Y	W	H	W	K	N
C	I	Z	F	L	Y	I	N	G
M	E	H	U	N	T	I	N	G
F	I	G	H	T	I	N	G	G
Z	P	J	U	M	P	I	N	G

2 Complete the sentences. Use the action words from Exercise 1.

1. I am _____jumping_____ out of the tree at the moment.

2. The tiger is _____ for food right now.

3. At the moment, the boy is _____ in the lake.

4. Tom is _____ in an airplane right now.

5. Now, Sheila is _____ on the swings on the playground.

6. Why are you _____ behind the tree?

7. The baby lions aren't _____. They're playing.

3. How do these animals travel? Match the animals to the verbs.

1. frogs   a. fly
2. zebras   b. swim
3. snakes   c. swing
4. monkeys   d. jump
5. fish   e. slide
6. birds   f. run

4 Look at the pictures. Correct the sentences.

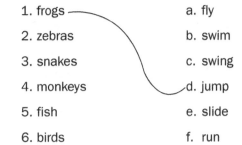

swimming
1. The boy is ~~hunting~~.

2. The girl is flying.

3. The boys are hiding.

4. The girls are jumping.

5. The birds are eating.

1 Complete the rules with *simple present* or *present continuous*.

> 1. To talk about facts, habits, and routines, we use the _____.
>
> 2. To talk about an action that is happening now, we use the _____.
>
> 3. We use *always*, *usually*, *sometimes*, and *never* with the _____.
>
> 4. We use *now* and *at the moment* with the _____ .

2 Circle the correct forms of the verbs.

Suncoast Seabird Sanctuary

Hi, my name is Sue. Right now, I ¹**work** / **'m working**
at the Suncoast Seabird Sanctuary during my school
vacation. It's a great job! About 10,000 birds
²**come** / **are coming** here each year. At the moment,
we ³**look** / **'re looking** after more than one hundred
birds! Suncoast is near the sea, so we have a lot of
sea birds. This is my favorite bird, Billy. He has a bad
wing, so the vet ⁴**looks** / **is looking** at him now.
I ⁵**feed** / **am feeding** Billy fish. A lot of people
⁶**visit** / **are visiting** the sanctuary every year,
especially in the summer. We always ⁷**explain** / **are
explaining** what we do to help the birds. We're open
every day. Come and visit us!

3 Write the correct forms of the verbs.

swim

1. In this photo, three dolphins
_____ next to our boat!

2. Dolphins _____ very fast,
up to 25 miles an hour.

lie

3. Cows usually _____ down in
the same direction when it rains.

4. Look! The cows in that field
_____ down.

eat

5. Large spiders _____ frogs
and other small animals.

6. Oh! The cat _____ our
dinner.

play

7. Today, _____ with my
uncle's dog, Patch.

8. I always _____ with Patch
on the weekend.

**4 Complete the sentences with the simple present
or present continuous of the verbs and your own
ideas.**

1. On the weekend, I usually
_____*do my homework*_____ . (do)

2. At the moment, I _____.
(read)

3. My friends and I sometimes
_____. (go)

4. Right this minute, I _____.

1 Put the words in order to make sentences.

1. do / get / I/ How / to / bird exhibit / the / ?

   _____How do I get to the bird exhibit?_____

2. down / Walk / hall / the / your / left / to / .

   _____

3. on / Is / it / the /floor / second / ?

   _____

4. Yes, it is. / a / Take / at / stairs / top / right / the / the / of / .

   _____

5. Then turn left. / down/ on / the hall / the right / It's / .

   _____

2 Help the boys from Exercise 1 find the polar bear exhibit. Complete the sentences to give them directions.

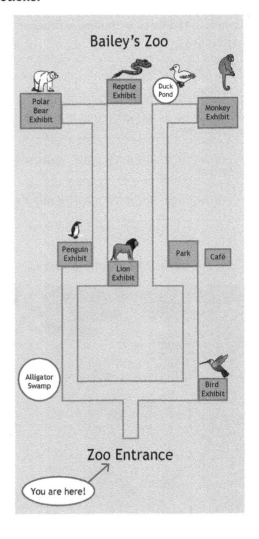

Bailey's Zoo

1. _____Go into the zoo entrance and take a left._____

2. Take a right at the _____.

3. _____ at the penguin exhibit.

4. Take a left at the _____.

5. At the reptile exhibit, _____

6. The polar bear exhibit is

   _____.

3 Now write directions from the zoo entrance to the monkey exhibit. Write six sentences.

1. _____

2. _____

3. _____

4. _____

5. _____

6. _____

✏️ READING TO WRITE

1 Complete the word web with the information.

Food

Looks

My Animal

hippopotamus

Location

Interesting Facts

Activities

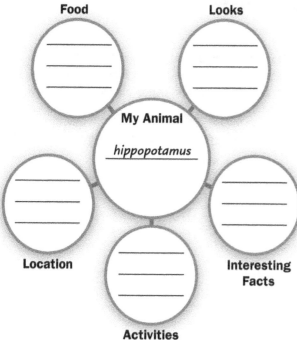

huge head

Africa

~~hippopotamus~~

lives in warm rivers and lakes

weighs up to 7,000 pounds

short neck

can run faster than a person

at night, climbs out of water and eats grass

long, round body

34 to 36 huge teeth

sleeps standing up in water during the day

different kinds of fish clean different parts of a hippo's body

strong, short legs

2 Put the words in order to make sentences about hippos. Then circle the adjectives.

1. large / are / Hippos / animals / very / .

_____*Hippos are very (large) animals.*_____

2. have / They / legs / strong / .

_____

3. have / Hippos / teeth / huge / .

_____

4. are / fast / Hippos / very / .

_____

5. sleep / rivers / in / They / warm / .

_____

3 Read the facts about polar bears. Then read the sentences. Are the sentences true (*T*) or false (*F*)?

FACTS ABOUT POLAR BEARS

live in the Arctic

hunt seals

have thick fur

paws up to 12 inches across

ears small and round

short tails

adult males weigh up to 1,200 pounds

adult females weigh up to 650 pounds

1. Polar bears live all over the world. ____*F*____

2. Polar bears have short tails and small, round ears. _____

3. Polar bears have large paws. _____

4. Male and female polar bears weigh the same. _____

5. Polar bears have very little fur. _____

8 City Life

VOCABULARY Places in town

1 Put the letters in the correct order to make places in town. Then match the words with the correct pictures.

a.

b.

c.

d.

e.

f.

g.

h.

i.

j.

1. MSKETUPRARE
   supermarket

2. TKASE ARPK
   _____

3. EFISNTS TECNRE
   _____

4. WLBOING LEYAL
   _____

5. IMUSTAD
   _____

6. MEUSUM
   _____

7. VIEMO EATHTER
   _____

8. AMLL
   _____

9. ARKMTE
   _____

10. RKAP
    _____

2 Put the places in town from Exercise 1 in the correct columns. Some places go in more than one column. Add other places in your town.

Indoor places	Outdoor places	Places to have fun	Places to exercise
supermarket			

3 Where can you do these things? Write places from Exercise 1.

1. watch a football game or see a concert
   stadium

2. buy some new jeans (2 places)
   _____   _____

3. go swimming or take a karate class
   _____

4. go on a field trip to learn about history
   _____

5. buy food (2 places)
   _____   _____

4 Complete the sentences with your own information.

1. I love going to
   the mall. The clothes are great!

2. I like going to
   _____

3. I never go to
   _____

4. On the weekend, I sometimes go to
   _____

5. I sometimes go to
   _____
   in another town.

GRAMMAR Simple past of *be* and *there was/were*

1 Circle the correct words.

1. I/He/She/It **was / were** there.
2. You/We/They **was / were** there.
3. He **wasn't / weren't** there.
4. **Was you / Were you** there?

2 Read the email. Circle the correct forms of *be*.

○○○

Hey Sam,

Yesterday, my dad and I went to the football stadium to see the Mavericks play the Chargers, but it ¹**wasn't / weren't** much fun. My favorite team, the Chargers, lost by a lot. It ²**was / were** hard to watch my team lose. They ³**wasn't / weren't** nearly as good as the other team. My team ⁴**wasn't / weren't** playing well. My dad and I ⁵**wasn't / weren't** happy that they lost so badly.

⁶**Was / Were** you watching the game on TV? Did you think it ⁷**was / were** fun? What's your favorite team this year? I know last year it ⁸**was / were** the Mavericks.

Your friend,

Tyler

3 Complete the sentences with the correct forms of *there was* and *there were*.

1. In 2013, ___*there were*___ many tourists in our town because of the new museum and stadium.

2. Before the new museum and stadium opened, _____ many people who visited here.

3. Last week _____ an exhibit at the museum. _____ a lot of people there to meet a famous artist.

4. _____ an important game at the stadium last Saturday?

5. The stadium was full. _____ any seats left.

4 Complete the questions with *was* or *were*. Then answer the questions.

1. Where _____*were*_____ you yesterday afternoon at three o'clock?

   ___*I was at home doing my homework.*___

2. What _____ your favorite TV show when you _____ younger?

   _____

3. How old _____ you in 2010?

   _____

4. How many students _____ there in your class last year?

   _____

5. _____ you out of school yesterday?

   _____

6. _____ there a test yesterday?

   _____

VOCABULARY Transportation places and prepositions of place

1 Label the places in the city. Correct the sentences to match the map.

1. The subway station is across the street from the market.

   The subway station is across the street from

   Tom's Restaurant.

2. The bus stop is behind the movie theater.

   _____

3. The girl is in front of the subway station.

   _____

4. The boy is behind the market.

   _____

5. The market is across the street from Carl's Coffee Café and the movie theater.

   _____

6. The woman is behind Tom's restaurant.

   _____

7. The bus station is behind the parking lot.

   _____

8. Sally's Shoe Shop is next to Mel's Market.

   _____

2 Complete the paragraph.

airport	ferry port	~~subway~~	train
bus stop	parking lot	taxi	

My family lives in the city. My mom works downtown. She takes an underground train called a [1] _____subway_____ . My dad works outside the city. He takes a [2] _____, too, but it's not underground. He leaves his car in the [3] _____ at the station. I wait for the bus at the [4] _____ each morning to go to school.

Every year, we fly to Washington to visit my grandparents. We don't have a car, so we ride in a [5] _____ to the [6] _____ to get on the plane. My grandparents live on an island called Mercer Island. After we get off the plane, we go to the [7] _____ to get a boat to the island.

GRAMMAR Simple past with regular and irregular verbs

1 Write the simple past forms of the regular verbs.

1. watch ___watched___
2. shop _____
3. wait _____
4. study _____
5. play _____
6. visit _____
7. like _____

2 Complete the sentences with the simple past form of the verbs.

1. Roman children ___played___ (play) board games.
2. We _____ (listen) to the concert at the stadium.
3. Katia and her friends _____ (wait) for the bus.
4. My family _____ (live) in the city last year.
5. They _____ (shop) at the mall.
6. We _____ (stay) at the bowling alley after 9:00 p.m.

3 Rewrite the sentences to make them negative. Use contractions.

1. My family watched the football game on TV.

   ___My family didn't watch the football game on TV.___

2. They visited the museum on their vacation.

   _____

3. We shopped at the mall for new shoes.

   _____

4. Jenna waited for her mom at the restaurant.

   _____

5. I studied for the test last night.

   _____

6. My brother played tennis in the park.

   _____

4 Write the simple past form of the irregular verbs.

1. see ___saw___
2. go _____
3. speak _____
4. fly _____
5. buy _____
6. take _____
7. understand _____

5 Complete the sentences with the correct form of the verbs.

do

1. Did you _____ anything fun at the park?
2. Yes, we _____. There were a lot of other kids to play with.

speak

3. Did you _____ in front of the class last week?
4. Yes, I _____ in front of all my classmates.

eat

5. Did you _____ at that new restaurant in the mall?
6. Yes, I _____ there. The food was great!

go

7. Did you _____ to the skate park three days ago?
8. No, I _____ to the mall.

CONVERSATION That sounds fun!

1 Complete the conversation.

Where did you go on vacation?	Can you believe it	Did you know that
Guess what	And that's not all	What else did you do
What	sounds fun	so cool

Katie: ¹ _____Where did you go on vacation?_____

Sally: My family and I went to Boston. We went to the Museum of Science and to Quincy Market.

Katie: Wow! That ² _____.

Sally: Yeah. ³ _____.

Katie: ⁴ _____?

Sally: Well, we did something really awesome! ⁵ _____ we did.

Katie: I don't know. ⁶ _____?

Sally: We went to the Top of the Hub Restaurant. It's 52 floors high!

Katie: That's ⁷ _____!

Sally: And after dinner we took a walk. ⁸ _____ it has a skywalk?
⁹ _____? We could see all of Boston from up there!

2 Write four more words to describe an exciting time.

1. _____ _amazing_ _____

2. _____

3. _____

4. _____

5. _____

To	Jason
From	Francesca
Subject	My trip to Hawaii

Hi Jason,

How was your vacation? My trip to Hawaii was great! My family and I landed at the airport on the "Big Island." It is about the size of the state of Connecticut. The state of Hawaii has hundreds of islands, but there are eight big islands. Hawaii became the last state of the United States in 1950. It's also the only state made up of islands! And the only state not located in the Americas. It is in Polynesia in the central Pacific Ocean.

We saw amazing waterfalls and went to Hawaii Volcanoes National Park and saw the active volcano, Kilauea. We went swimming and surfing, too. The beaches are beautiful!

On our last night, we went to a *luau*, a Hawaiian party. We ate *poi*, a kind of plant, and also some delicious fish. We listened to Hawaiian music and watched a dance called the *hula*, too.

I didn't want to come home! I can't wait to hear about your vacation!

Your friend,

Francesca

1 Read Francesca's email. Complete the word web.

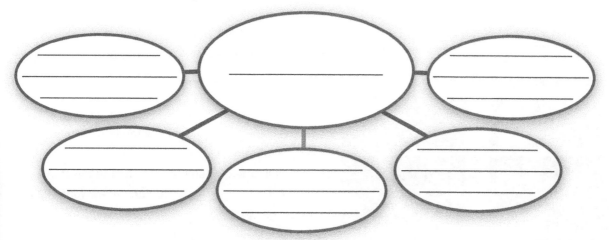

2 Circle examples of *also* and *too* in Francesca's email.

3 Rewrite the sentences using *too* or *also*.

1. My brother and I flew to Chicago this summer. (New York / too)
   We flew to New York, too.

2. I went to the zoo yesterday. (beach / also)
   _____

3. Sally is studying for her math test. (history test / too)
   _____

4. Jim and Michael are going to ride their bikes. (go swimming / too)
   _____

1 Match the descriptions to the correct pictures. Then write the names of the places.

1. a place to wait for a taxi _____

   _____

2. a place to buy groceries _____

   _____

3. an animal that lives on a farm _____

   _____

4. a place to learn about art and history _____

   _____

5. an animal with a very long neck _____

   _____

6. a place to watch a concert _____

   _____

7. a place to take a boat _____

   _____

8. a place to lift weights _____

   _____

9. an animal that lives in the Arctic _____

   _____

10. a place to leave a car _____

    _____

a

b

c

d

e

f

g

h

i

j

2 Complete the sentences with the simple present, present continuous, or simple past of the verbs.

1. I _____ (go) to the bus station yesterday.

2. I usually _____ (take) a taxi to the airport.

3. Tom and Lila _____ (visit) the museum now.

4. She _____ (speak) to her brother last night at the train station.

5. Tim always _____ (ride) a bus to work.

6. Sera and Fran _____ (eat) lunch at the moment.

3 Circle the correct answers.

1. _____ a lot of birds flying over the lake yesterday.

   a. There are   b. There were

2. No, the tiger _____ in the jungle right now.

   a. isn't hunting   b. didn't hunt

3. _____ ducks at the pond today?

   a. Are there   b. There were

4. Petra, Angkor, and Tanis _____ small towns in the past.

   a. were   b. are

5. I _____ Hawaii with my family last winter.

   a. visited   b. is visiting

6. _____ many tourists there when we went.

   a. There wasn't   b. There weren't

7. I _____ to Paris a few years ago.

   a. am flying   b. flew

8. My parents usually _____ home on Saturdays.

   a. stay   b. are staying

4 Complete the sentences with the correct forms of the verbs. Write simple present, present continuous, or simple past.

fight	hunt	swim
hide	~~jump~~	playing

1. The frogs ___are jumping___ from rock to rock no
   ____present continuous____

2. The tigers _____ in the jungle last night for their meal. _____

3. At the moment, those angry cats _____ with each other. _____

4. Sharks always _____ in the sea. _____

5. The spiders _____ inside the tree right now. _____

6. The cute puppies _____ with a ball yesterday. _____

5 Put the words in the correct order to ask for and give directions.

1. can / I / Where / find / the / ferry port / ?

_____

2. on the way / to / fish market / the / It's / .

_____

3. the corner / Go up / the stairs / and / turn right / at / .

_____

4. Take a / bus stop / in front of / the / left / .

_____

5. Turn right / at / mall / the / and / then / straight / go / .

_____

6 Answer the questions about your favorite animal. Write complete sentences.

1. What is your favorite animal?

_____

2. Where does it live?

_____

3. What does it look like?

_____

4. What does it eat?

_____

7 Answer the questions about your favorite place. Write complete sentences.

1. What is your favorite place?

_____

2. Where is it?

_____

3. What does it look like?

_____

4. What do you like to do there?

_____

8 Complete the conversation.

> I can't wait to see them
> I can't wait to see you
> That sounds so beautiful
> What fun things did you do there
> What else did you do

Janet: Hello?

Stella: Hi, Janet! It's Stella. How are you? Guess what! Last month, I flew to Paris with my mom. What an amazing vacation!

Janet: ¹_____?

Stella: We saw the Mona Lisa in the Louvre Museum, and we went to the Eiffel Tower.

Janet: ²_____?

Stella: We also took a boat ride down the Seine at night and saw Paris with all its lights!

Janet: ³_____!

Stella: It was. We also ate a lot of delicious food, and I bought some cool clothes at a street market. I put my photos online so you and my other friends can see my amazing trip.

Janet: ⁴_____!

Stella: We had a fantastic time. I have a lot more to tell you. And I want to hear about your vacation, too!

Janet: ⁵_____! When can we get together?

Fun and Games

VOCABULARY Sports and activities

1 Use the pictures to complete the crossword.

Down

 1 ✓
 2
 4
 5

 7
 9

Across

 2
 3
 6
 8

 10
 11

2 Complete the word web with the sports from Exercise 1.

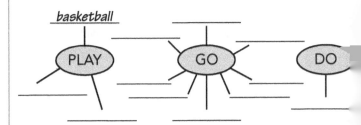

basketball

PLAY   GO   DO

3 Complete the paragraph with the sports words from Exercise 1.

I love water sports! I go ¹ _____swimming_____ in the pool a lot. But I don't live near the ocean, so I don't go ² _____ or ³ _____. I don't like snow, so I don't go ⁴ _____ or ⁵ _____. I like sports you play with teams. I like playing ⁶ _____, ⁷ _____, and ⁸ _____. I just started doing ⁹ _____. It's fun, but I'm not very good yet. I'm only a white belt. I got a new bike for my birthday, so now my favorite thing to do is to go ¹⁰ _____ in the park with my friends. Sometimes I also go ¹¹ _____ in the park. On rainy days, I go ¹² _____.

4 Which sports do you like? Write at least three sentences. Use the ideas below or your own ideas.

boring	easy for me
dangerous	fun
difficult for me	scary

1. *I think bowling is fun, but it is difficult for me.*
2. _____
3. _____
4. _____

GRAMMAR Simple past *yes/no* questions and short answers

1 Complete the text with the negative simple past form of the verbs.

buy	go
eat	see
~~go~~	win

Yesterday was Saturday, so I ¹ ___*didn't go*___ to school.
I got up very late, so I ² _____ any breakfast,
just lunch. Then I went shopping, but I ³ _____
anything good, so I ⁴ _____ anything.
My parents went bowling last night, but my brother Mike
and I ⁵ _____. We stayed home and watched
a baseball game on TV. Our team ⁶ _____.

2 Complete the questions about Exercise 1. Then answer the questions with short answers.

1. Q: _____*Did you go*_____ (you / go) to school yesterday?

   A: _____*No, I didn't.*_____

2. Q: _____ (you / get) up very late?

   A: _____

3. Q: _____ (you / eat) any lunch?

   A: _____

4. Q: _____ (you / buy) anything when you went shopping?

   A: _____

5. Q: _____ (your parents / go) bowling last night?

   A: _____

6. Q: _____ (you and Mike / stay) home last night?

   A: _____

7. Q: _____ (you and Mike / watch) soccer on TV?

   A: _____

8. Q: _____ (your team / win) yesterday?

   A: _____

3 Write affirmative (✓) and negative (✗) sentences in the simple past.

1. I (ride) my bike last night. (✗)

   _____*I didn't ride my bike last night.*_____

2. My cousins (go) snowboarding last week. (✓)

   _____

3. Tracy and I (play) volleyball this morning. (✓)

   _____

4. John (watch) a movie yesterday. (✗)

   _____

5. Mary (do) judo last night. (✗)

   _____

6. Harry and I (play) baseball last summer. (✓)

   _____

7. Justin (study) for his test this morning. (✓)

   _____

8. I (speak) to my friend last night. (✗)

   _____

9. He (eat) a big breakfast yesterday. (✗)

   _____

10. Cathy (make) her bed this morning. (✓)

   _____

4 Answer these questions about you.

1. Did you go skiing this year?

   _____*No, I didn't.*_____

2. Did you play basketball last week?

   _____

3. Did you watch TV yesterday?

   _____

4. Did you go bowling last winter?

   _____

1 Put the letters in order to make clothes words.

1. STTARCKIUT _____tracksuit_____

2. SEWASRITTH _____

3. STHRIT- _____

4. NTPAS _____

5. OTOBS _____

6. TRIKS _____

7. SKOSC _____

8. DEOHOI _____

9. PAC _____

10. KEJCAT _____

11. EJASN _____

12. TRSHOS _____

2 Circle the words that don't belong.

1. jeans	pants	(boots)
2. sweatshirt	T-shirt	socks
3. sneakers	boots	skirt
4. dress	skirt	cap
5. hoodie	sweatshirt	dress
6. T-shirt	socks	sneakers
7. jacket	shorts	hoodie

3 Circle the correct answers.

1. People usually don't wear _____ in very hot weather.

   a. a sweatshirt   b. sneakers   c. shorts

2. Jenna wears _____ to play volleyball.

   a. a jacket   b. shorts   c. boots

3. In the Olympics, runners wear _____ before the race.

   a. tracksuits   b. socks   c. a cap

4. Mary wears _____ to hike.

   a. a skirt   b. boots   c. a dress

5. In the winter, I wear _____ over my shirt.

   a. a cap   b. a jacket   c. socks

4 Read your activities for tomorrow. Plan your clothes. It is very cold in the morning. Later in the day, it is warmer.

6:00 a.m. go running outside	sneakers
8:00 a.m. go to school	
3:00 p.m. play tennis outside	
6:00 p.m. go out to dinner	

GRAMMAR Simple past
Wh- questions

1 Match the questions to the correct answers.

1. Who did you go windsurfing with?	a. Yesterday afternoon.
2. Where did you read that?	b. Karla and Sammie.
3. When did you go skiing?	c. In the newspaper.
4. How many miles did we ride?	d. My new jacket.
5. How did you get to the store?	e. Almost 20.
6. What did you wear?	f. By car.

2 Complete the questions.

1. _____ did you do yesterday?

   We went windsurfing.

2. _____ did you go windsurfing?

   We went to Malibu Beach.

3. _____ did you go?

   We went in the early afternoon.

4. _____ did you get to the beach?

   We went by car.

5. _____ long did you windsurf?

   We windsurfed for a couple of hours.

3 Complete the chart with information from the paragraph.

> Karen and her best friend, Carrie, went to Mount Kemo in New Hampshire yesterday. They went by bus with some people from their ski club. They wore their new ski jackets and ski boots. They got there early in the morning. They skied all morning. At noon they had a big lunch. They were very hungry after so much exercise. After lunch they went snowboarding. They were tired on the way home. They fell asleep on the bus.

What?	*went skiing and snowboarding*
Who?	
Where?	
How?	
When?	

4 Complete the Wh- questions and about Exercise 3. Answer the questions.

1. Q: _____*What did*_____ Karen and Carrie ____*wear*____ ?

   A: _____

2. Q: _____ they get there?

   A: _____ early in the morning.

3. Q: _____ they _____ lunch?

   A: _____

4. Q: _____ they _____ after lunch?

   A: _____

5. Q: _____ they _____ asleep?

   A: _____

1 Put the sentences in order to make a conversation.

_1_	Michael:	What did you do on vacation, Todd?
____	Michael:	Cool! How was that?
____	Todd:	I went snowboarding.
____	Michael:	Really? That's too bad.
____	Todd:	I kept losing the board. I had to run down the mountain after it.
____	Michael:	Now, that sounds like fun!
____	Todd:	Yeah, but after a while, I learned to stay on and even turn. I loved flying across the snow.
____	Todd:	It was really great! At first, I didn't think I could do it. I had a lot of problems.
____	Michael:	Why? What happened?

2 Circle the phrases in Exercise 1 that express interest.

3 Match the questions to the answers.

1. Where did you go on vacation?

2. What else did you do?

3. Why? What happened?

4. Cool! How was that?

a. It was amazing flying in a helicopter over the park!

b. I lost my family hiking on one of the trails, but I finally found them.

c. My family and I went to Yosemite National Park in California.

d. We also went skiing.

1 Read Melissa Franklin's biography. Then complete the timeline of important events in her life.

Melissa "Missy" Franklin was born(in)1995 in Pasadena, California, and grew up in Centennial, Colorado. She started swimming when she was five years old. In 2009, at age 14, Missy won her first international swim event. In the 2012 Olympics in London, Missy swam in seven different events and won three gold medals. She set the Olympic record in the backstroke and became the fastest woman ever. In 2013, she became a student at the University of California in Berkeley. She swims on the swim team there. She wants to go to the next Olympics.

Missy was born.

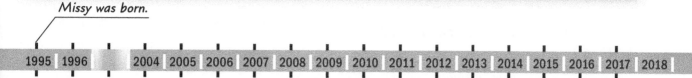

| 1995 | 1996 | | 2004 | 2005 | 2006 | 2007 | 2008 | 2009 | 2010 | 2011 | 2012 | 2013 | 2014 | 2015 | 2016 | 2017 | 2018 |

2 Circle the prepositions of time and underline the prepositions of place in Melissa Franklin's biography.

3 Read the biography again. Answer the questions. Write complete sentences.

1. When was Melissa Franklin born?

   _____ *She was born in 1995.* _____

2. Where was Melissa Franklin born?

   _____

3. When did Melissa Franklin win her first international swim event?

   _____

4. When did Melissa Franklin swim in the London Olympics?

   _____

5. What did Melissa Franklin set a record in at the 2012 Olympics?

   _____

6. Where does Melissa Franklin go to school?

   _____

10 Vacation: Here and There

1 Find seven more weather words.

S	T	O	R	M	Y	P	W	D
F	O	G	G	Y	F	H	C	Z
I	H	A	L	S	U	N	N	Y
C	R	A	I	N	Y	O	O	B
Y	P	S	N	O	W	Y	J	H
F	N	G	W	I	N	D	Y	Q
F	W	S	P	X	D	O	H	C
W	I	C	L	O	U	D	Y	S
T	M	X	A	O	X	H	P	I

2 Complete the sentences. Use the words from Exercise 1.

Hello! Here is today's world weather:

1. At the moment in Kingston, Jamaica, it's the _____*rainy*_____ season. Today there's a lot of rain, and it's very _____*stormy*_____.

2. In London today, the weather is 12°C. It's gray and _____, but you don't need your umbrella — it isn't _____.

3. In Ottawa it's cold (–1°C) and very _____. People are making snowmen.

4. Today in San Francisco, it's very _____. You can't see anything, so drive carefully.

5. In Helsinki, it's –2°C today. It's cold and _____, so it's a good day to skate!

6. In Rio de Janeiro today it's beach weather. It's hot (28°C) and _____.

3 Circle the correct answers.

> Jim lives in Connecticut, where there are four seasons. In the winter months, [1]_____, it's cold and [2]_____. He likes to ski and [3]_____. In the spring, [4]_____, it gets warm and [5]_____. Jim plays on the [6]_____ team at school. In the summer months, [7]_____, it's hot and [8]_____. Jim's favorite summer activities are swimming and playing [9]_____. But Jim's favorite season is fall, [10]_____. It's beginning to get [11]_____, but there are many beautiful, sunny days. He plays [12]_____ in fall.

1. (a.) December–February
   b. March–May
   c. June–August

2. a. hot   b. warm   c. snowy

3. a. windsurf   b. snowboard   c. swim

4. a. June–August
   b. March–May
   c. September–November

5. a. windy   b. snowy   c. icy

6. a. snowboarding b. baseball   c. skiing

7. a. March–May

   b. June–August

   c. September–November

8. a. sunny   b. snowy   c. cold

9. a. tennis   b. kung fu   c. windsurfing

10. a. March–May

    b. June–August

    c. September–November

11. a. warm   b. cold   c. snowy

12. a. football   b. judo   c. bowling

GRAMMAR   *be going to*

1 Circle the correct words.

1. **He's going to buy / He buys** a camera tomorrow.

2. We **are going to eat / eat** dinner at seven o'clock every night.

3. A: **Are you going to watch / Do you watch** TV tonight?

   B: Yes, **I'm going / I am.**

2 Look at the pictures. What are the people going to do? Complete the sentences with *be going to*.

Amanda

Cristina and me

Me

Lucas

Alicia and Robin

You and your family

1. _____*Lucas is going to*_____ learn to ride a horse.

2. _____ be famous movie stars.

3. _____ climb Mount Everest.

4. _____ buy a laptop.

5. _____ live in the country.

6. _____ travel around the world.

3 Complete the sentences. Use *be going to*.

1. What _____*are you going to do*_____ (do) now that you finished your homework?

2. When _____ you _____ (visit) your parents?

3. I think my brother _____ (buy) a new MP3 player.

4. I _____ (take) a shower after I exercise.

5. We _____ (not tell) you that!

4 Read the questions. Write "No" answers. Use *be going to* and the activities. Use contractions.

1. Are you going to study for your history test tonight? (study for your French test)

   No, I'm not. I'm going to study for my French test tonight.

2. Are Sally and Missy going to go swimming tomorrow? (play tennis)

   _____

3. Is Paula going to go bowling Saturday? (go windsurfing)

   _____

4. Is Ralph going to visit his grandparents this weekend? (visit his cousins)

   _____

5. Are you going to go snowboarding during vacation? (go skiing)

   _____

VOCABULARY Landforms

1 Write the name of each landform under its picture.

1. an _____

2. a _____

3. a _____

4. a _____

5. a _____

6. a _____

7 a _____

8. a _____

9 a _____

2 Write the landforms in Exercise 1 in the correct columns.

Bodies of water	Bodies of land
ocean	

3 Circle the word that doesn't belong.

1. mountain	lake	hill
2. jungle	lake	ocean
3. forest	jungle	river
4. ocean	desert	beach

4 Complete the sentences. Use the words in the box. There are some extra words.

beach	jungle	~~mountain~~	river
desert	lake	ocean	

1. We got a lot of exercise hiking up and down the _____mountain_____ .

2. We went down the _____ in a boat.

3. A tiger is an animal that lives in the _____.

4. We made a castle in the sand at the _____.

5. The Atlantic is an _____, and so is the Pacific.

GRAMMAR Superlatives

1 Complete the rules and write the superlative forms of the adjectives.

1. For most adjectives with one syllable, add _____-est_____ .

   long → _____longest_____

2. For most adjectives with two or more syllables, add _____.

   popular → _____

3. For most adjectives ending in consonant + -y, change the ending to _____.

   rainy → _____

4. Some adjectives are irregular:

   good → _____

   bad → _____

2 Write the comparative and superlative forms of the adjectives.

	Comparative	Superlative
tall	*taller*	*tallest*
colorful		
good		
bad		
important		
icy		
beautiful		
popular		

3 Read the information about deserts. Complete the sentences. Use information from the chart.

	Size	Average rainfall	Average temperature
Sahara Desert	3,600,000 sq. miles (9,323,957 sq. km)	3 inches (7.62 cm)	High: 100°F (38°C) Low: 50°F (10°C)
Gobi Desert	500,000 sq. miles (1,294,994 sq. km)	7.6 inches (19.4 cm)	High: 66°F (19°C) Low: 2°F (-17°C)
Arctic Desert	5,405,432 sq. miles (14,000,005 sq. km)	20 inches (51 cm)	High: 50°F (10°C) Low: -32°F (-36°C)
Kalahari Desert	220,000 sq. miles (569,797 sq. km)	2 inches (5.08 cm)	High: 104° F (40°C) Low: 77°F (25°C)

1. The Arctic Desert is the ____*biggest*____ desert.

   It is ____*bigger*____ than the Sahara Desert.

2. The Kalahari is the _____ desert.

   It is _____ than the Gobi Desert.

3. The Arctic gets the _____ rainfall.

   It is the _____ desert.

4. The Kalahari gets the _____ rainfall.

   It is the _____ desert.

5. The Arctic Desert has the _____ temperature. It is much _____ than the Kalahari Desert.

6. The Sahara has the _____ temperature. It is much _____ than the Arctic Desert.

4 Look at the pictures. Write four more sentences using comparative and superlative adjectives.

parrot

hippo

dolphin

rabbit

goat

1. _____*The rabbit has the longest ears.*_____

2. _____

3. _____

4. _____

5. _____

5 Answer these questions with your own information. Use superlative adjectives.

1. The _____ (old) person in my family is my _____.

2. The _____ (young) person in my family is _____.

3. The _____ (funny) movie I've ever seen is _____.

4. The _____ (pretty) actress is _____.

5. The _____ (popular) food at my house is _____.

6. The _____ (intelligent) person in my family is _____.

1 **Put the sentences in order to make a conversation. Write the numbers. Then read the conversation again and circle the suggestions.**

_____	**Debbie:**	No. It's too cold to swim. We can go on the roller coaster instead.
_____	**Tania:**	Good plan! But why don't we get something to eat first?
_____	**Tania:**	I don't know. Roller coasters are really scary. What about going windsurfing?
_1_	**Tania:**	Let's go swimming!
_____	**Tania:**	Me too. We can eat and then go windsurfing. It's going to be a wonderful day!
_____	**Debbie:**	Good idea. I'm really hungry!
_____	**Debbie:**	Hmm . . . It's windy today, so it's a good day for it. OK. Let's do that!

2 **Complete the conversation with your own ideas. Use the phrases in the box.**

how about	we can
let's	why don't we

1. **A:** Let's go swimming.
   B: It's too cold.
   A: _____ *Let's go to the movies.* _____
2. **A:** Let's have lunch.
   B: I'm not hungry.
   A: _____
3. **A:** How about riding our bikes?
   B: I'm tired.
   A: _____
4. **A:** Why don't we go skiing?
   B: There's not much snow.
   A: _____
5. **A:** How about playing tennis?
   B: It's too hot.
   A: _____
6. **A:** Let's go windsurfing.
   B: But, it's not windy.
   A: _____

1   Read the email and complete the chart.

To   jenm@net.cup.org
From   sashap@net.cup.org
Subject   My trip to New York City

Thanks for your email! And thanks for the photos of your vacation. It looks like you had lots of fun.

I'm going to go on vacation the last week in June. I'm going to New York City. I'm going to fly there with my mom, dad, and sister. We're going to stay in a fancy hotel near Central Park. Since it's going to be warm, I'm going to skate and cycle in the park.

We're going to visit Ellis Island and the Statue of Liberty. We're going to see the city from the top of the Empire State Building! And I'm going to see the musical *Matilda*. I can't wait!

I hope everything is good with you. Write me soon.

Your friend,

Sasha

Sasha's Vacation	
1. Where is she going to go?	Sasha is going to go to _____.
2. When is she going to go?	She is going to go the last week in _____.
3. What's the weather going to be like?	It is going to be _____.
4. Who is she going to go with?	Sasha is going to go with her _____, _____, and _____.
5. How is she going to get there?	She is going to _____ there.
6. Where is she going to stay?	Sasha is going to stay at a fancy _____ near Central Park.
7. What is she going to see and do?	Sasha is going to visit the Statue of Liberty, _____, and the Empire State Building. She is going to see the _____ *Matilda*, and she is going to _____ and _____ in Central Park.

2   Read the sentences to start and end an email. Write the sentences in the correct column.

Please write back soon.	How are your parents?
Thanks for your email.	I got your email, thanks.
I hope you're well.	How are you?
What are you going to do next summer?	When are you going to go on vacation?

Start an email	End an email

1 Circle the correct answers.

Alice: I love ¹**winter / summer / fall** because it's hot and ²**snowy / sunny / icy**. It's the ³**most hot / more hot / hottest** season of the year. It's a good time to go ⁴**windsurfing / snowboarding / ice skating** and swimming.

Ben: I like ⁵**winter / spring / summer** because it's ⁶**cold / warm / hot** and sometimes snowy. It's a good time to go ⁷**snowboarding / windsurfing / swimming**, and skiing. It's the ⁸**colder / most cold / coldest** season of the year.

Tammy: I love ⁹**winter / spring / summer** because it is ¹⁰**icy / foggy / warm** and I can play baseball. I need my umbrella a lot because it's the ¹¹**foggiest / rainiest / most windy** season.

Pam: I love ¹²**spring / winter / fall** because the leaves are the ¹³**more colorful / most colorful / colorful** of any season. I think it's the ¹⁴**most pretty / prettiest / prettier** season of the year. It is cool outside. I can wear my ¹⁵**hoodie / shorts / T-shirt** playing basketball.

2 Write the names of the landforms.

| beach | jungle | mountains | river |
| hill | lake | ocean | |

1 _____ 2 _____

3 _____ 4 _____ 5 _____

6 _____ 7 _____

3 Match the questions with the correct answers.

1. Where is he going to go tomorrow?
2. Did he hike in the mountains yesterday?
3. When did he leave the beach yesterday?
4. What did he wear yesterday?
5. Are Brent and Ted going to wrestle tomorrow?
6. How many points did she get?

a. No, he didn't.
b. Shorts and a T-shirt.
c. To the desert.
d. Yes, they are.
e. Ten.
f. At noon.

4 Choose the correct answers.

1. **A:** _____ did Karen visit yesterday?
   a. Who   b. How   c. When
   B: She _____ her mom.
   a. is going to visit   b. visited   c. visits

2. **A:** Is Tim _____ to the beach today?
   a. going to go   b. went   c. will go
   B: No, he _____.
   a. isn't   b. didn't   c. doesn

3. **A:** _____ you see your friends yesterday?
   a. Do   b. Did   c. Does
   B: Yes, I _____.
   a. do   b. didn't   c. did

4. **A:** Are they _____ later today?
   a. going to study   b. studied   c. studi
   B: No, they _____.
   a. aren't   b. didn't   c. don't

5. **A:** _____ did you cycle last weekend?
   a. Where   b. When   c. Why
   B: I _____ to the beach.
   a. cycled   b. am going to cycle c. cyclir

6. **A:** Where is Tim _____ on his vacatio next week?
   a. go   b. going to go   c. wen
   B: He _____ to the mountains.
   a. is going to go   b. are going   c. goes

5 Write *yes/no* questions and answers with *be going to* or the simple past.

1. Tom / play soccer / yesterday (no, basketball)
   Q: _____Did Tom play soccer yesterday?_____
   A: _____No, he played basketball._____

2. Tom and Mack / bowling / tomorrow? (yes)
   Q: _____
   A: _____

3. Jim / surfing / last summer? (no, snorkeling)
   Q: _____
   A: _____

4. You / swimming / next Saturday? (no, cycling)
   Q: _____
   A: _____

5. You / to Spain / last year (yes)
   Q: _____
   A: _____

6 Rewrite the sentences to make them correct.

1. Why don't we visiting the Tokyo?

   _____

2. What about go to the forest instead?

   _____

3. Jerry go to the sports event at June 2013.

   _____

4. We go swimming every day last summer.

   _____

5. I like summer because it is the hotter season.

   _____

6. Fall is the more beautiful season of the year.

   _____

7 Complete the conversations. Some of the words and phrases will be used more than once.

amazing	Let's	What did
cool	Really	Why don't
How was	What about	

1. **A:** _____ wear our new hoodies to play basketball.

   B: _____ we wear our sports jackets instead?

2. **A:** _____ go to Canada on vacation.

   B: It's too cold there in winter.

   _____ go to Hawaii.

3. **A:** _____ you do during your vacation?

   B: We went skydiving. It was

   _____!

4. **A:** _____ go skiing at Mount Kemo.

   B: _____? Isn't that too far away?

5. **A:** _____ your trip to Mexico last month?

   B: It was so _____!

6. **A:** _____ we travel to Europe?

   B: It's too far. _____ going to California instead?

8 Read the paragraph. Decide whether the sentences are true (*T*) or false (*F*).

Calvin likes to go running outside in the cold winter months. He wears his warmest tracksuit. As the winter season turns to spring and the weather is not as cold, Calvin likes to play tennis. He plays tennis in shorts and his hoodie. In the warm summer months, Calvin goes skateboarding a lot. He wears shorts, a T-shirt, and a baseball cap. Calvin plays soccer in the fall. He wears shorts and his favorite soccer shirt. On colder fall days, he wears a sweatshirt over his shirt.

1. Calvin likes to run in the winter. _____T_____

2. Calvin likes to play baseball in the spring.

   _____

3. He plays tennis in shorts and a hoodie.

   _____

4. Calvin wears a baseball cap to go skateboarding.

   _____

5. Calvin plays soccer in the summer. _____

6. Calvin wears a tracksuit to play soccer.

   _____

Anuj's FIRST DAY

BEFORE YOU WATCH

1 Look at the picture from the video. Circle the correct words.

1. This **is** / **are** a school in India.

2. The boys **is** / **are** students.

3. The students **is** / **are** in class.

4. The teacher **is** / **are** a man.

WHILE YOU WATCH

2 Watch the video. Are the sentences true (*T*) or false (*F*)? Correct the false sentences.

1. _____ Anuj is 12 years old.   _____

2. _____ Anuj eats breakfast with his teacher.   _____

3. _____ The school is all girls.   _____

4. _____ The students study English.   _____

5. _____ The students live at the school.   _____

3 Watch the video again. When do these things happen? Write numbers 1 to 5.

_____ go to history class

_____ eat breakfast

_____ play games

_____ go to English class

_____ walk in the mountains

AFTER YOU WATCH

4 Work with a partner. Complete the chart about you and your school.

Your name	Your age	Your school's name	Your teacher's name
Peter	12	Harris School	Mr. Black

My name is Peter. I am 12 years old. I go to Harris School. My teacher's name is Mr. Black.

Jin Yang: A GYMNAST

BEFORE YOU WATCH

1 Look at the pictures from the video. Circle the correct words.

1. This girl is a great **gymnast / gymnastics**.

2. The girls in this **gymnast / gymnastics** class are 10 years old.

WHILE YOU WATCH

2 Watch the video. Are the sentences true (*T*) or false (*F*)? Correct the false sentences.

1. _____ Jin Yang lives with her father.   _____

2. _____ Gymnastics practice is every day.   _____

3. _____ Jin Yang sees her mother.   _____

4. _____ Jin Yang runs in the hallway.   _____

5. _____ Jin Yang loves the park.   _____

3 Watch the video again. Match the sentences with the correct words.

1. Jin Yang is 12 _____ old.   a. father

2. Her class is all _____.   b. difficult

3. Her teacher is a _____.   c. man

4. Jin Yang and her _____ are at the park.   d. years

5. The gymnastics class is very _____.   e. girls

AFTER YOU WATCH

4 Discuss: What club or sport do you like? Why?

> I like science. It's very interesting. I am in a science club at school.

> I like painting. I go to an art class every day after school.

The YELLOW FERRARI

BEFORE YOU WATCH

1 Look at the pictures. Circle the correct words.

1. This is Maria. She is **12 / 17 / 30** years old.

2. This is her **car / bike / boat**.

3. Maria's car is really **fast / slow / old**.

4. This is Maria's **brother / family / friend**.

WHILE YOU WATCH

2 Watch the video. Are the sentences true (*T*) or false (*F*)? Correct the false sentences.

1. _____ Maria lives in Spain.   _____

2. _____ Maria's car is blue.   _____

3. _____ Maria's favorite car is the Ferrari.   _____

4. _____ Maria is a student.   _____

5. _____ Maria is first in the race.   _____

3 Complete the sentences with the correct words.

1. Ferraris are _____ cars.

2. _____ is a city in Italy.

3. Maria's teacher is a _____.

4. Maria has an _____ race.

5. Maria's _____ goes to the race.

Italian
important
man
Rome
family

AFTER YOU WATCH

4 Work with a partner.

1. Work with a partner. Say a country. Your partner names a car from that country. Take turns.

Japan.   Toyota.

2. Discuss: What is your favorite car?

My favorite car is a Ford.

Young SCIENTISTS

BEFORE YOU WATCH

1 Look at the pictures. Complete the sentences with the correct words.

golf

laptop

scientists

1. I write my papers on my _____.

2. He is playing _____.

3. These _____ study chemistry.

WHILE YOU WATCH

2 Watch the video. Circle the correct answers.

1. The students are all from _____.
   a. Washington D.C.   b. Hawaii   c. the United States
2. They all love _____.
   a. golf   b. science   c. music
3. Jack's favorite sport is _____.
   a. tennis   b. soccer   c. golf
4. Michael's favorite thing is a red _____.
   a. plane   b. train   c. phone
5. Melissa is a student and a _____.
   a. musician   b. teacher   c. tennis player

3 Watch the video again. Match the people with the places.

Who	Place
1. Jack _____	a. Missouri
2. Michael _____	b. Hawaii
3. Avni _____	c. Illinois
4. Melissa _____	d. Pennsylvania

AFTER YOU WATCH

4 Work with a partner. Complete the chart. Talk about your favorite things.

My favorite . . .

Country	City	Sport	Singer
Spain	*Madrid*	*soccer*	*Katy Perry*

My favorite country is Spain. My favorite city is Madrid. I love soccer. I really like Katy Perry!

Robot FIGHTERS

BEFORE YOU WATCH

1 Write the correct words next to the pictures from the video.

| daughter | father | mother | prizes | robot |

1. _____

2. _____

3. _____

4. _____

5. _____

WHILE YOU WATCH

2 Watch the video. Check (✓) the sentences you hear.

1. This is my uncle and his family. _____

2. This is my sister. _____

3. Hiroshi makes the prizes. _____

4. My aunt's robot is in the competition, too. _____

5. Arina gets a prize. _____

6. She's really tall! _____

3 Watch the video again. Are the sentences true (*T*) or false (*F*)? Correct the false sentences.

1. _____ The family lives in London.   _____

2. _____ Tokyo is in China.   _____

3. _____ The girl is 11 years old.   _____

4. _____ The girl loves video games.   _____

5. _____ The mother's robot has long, white hair. _____

6. _____ The mother and the daughter get a prize. _____

AFTER YOU WATCH

4 Work in small groups. Describe your family. What are their names? What do they like doing?

My father's name is David. He likes playing golf.
My mother's name is Mona. She likes reading.

My SIBERIAN FAMILY

BEFORE YOU WATCH

1 Match the words with the pictures from the video.

| Siberia | reindeer | Khanty people |

1. _____ 2. _____ 3. _____

2 Now complete the sentences with the words from the video.

_____ is in the north of Russia. My grandparents are _____. They have a lot of _____.

WHILE YOU WATCH

3 Watch the video. When do you see these things? Write numbers 1 to 5.

_____ the boy and his father

_____ the grandparents

_____ the reindeer

_____ the snowmobile

_____ the town

4 Watch the video again. Circle the correct answers.

1. Siberia is in _____.
   a. Norway   b. Russia   c. China
2. The grandparents have about _____ reindeer.
   a. 5   b. 15   c. 50
3. The boy's town is very _____.
   a. small   b. short   c. big
4. The town has _____ store(s).
   a. one   b. two   c. three
5. The boy and his father _____ at the grandparents' house.
   a. work   b. play   c. work and play

AFTER YOU WATCH

5 Work with a partner. Who is your favorite family member? Where does he or she live? Who does he or she live with?

> My favorite relative is my Aunt Hilda. She lives in Mexico City. She lives with my Uncle Carlos.

Ali's DAY

BEFORE YOU WATCH

1 Match the sentences with the pictures from the video.

a.    b.    c.

1. Cairo is a very big city in Egypt. _____

2. This is Ali at work. He makes bread in the mornings. _____

3. Ali takes bread to people on his bike. _____

WHILE YOU WATCH

2 Watch the video. Complete the sentences with the correct number.

5	6	7	15	17

1. Ali is _____ years old.

2. He works _____ hours a day.

3. He works _____ days a week.

4. He gets up at _____ o'clock every morning.

5. He goes to work at _____ o'clock.

3 Watch the video again. Circle the correct answers.

1. Where does Ali live?

   a. Istanbul   b. Cairo   c. Paris

2. What does he do during the day?

   a. takes flowers to people   b. plays tennis   c. makes bread

3. When does Ali take things to people?

   a. in the evening   b. in the morning and the afternoon   c. at midnight

4. Who does Ali eat with?

   a. his friends from work   b. his friends from school   c. his family

AFTER YOU WATCH

4 Work with a partner. Who in your family works? Say four things they do every day. When do they do them? Take turns.

> My mother works. She always gets up at 6:00. She eats breakfast at 7:00. She comes home at 5:00. She usually watches TV at night.

La QUINCEAÑERA

BEFORE YOU WATCH

1 Match the words with the correct pictures.

| dance | dress | ring | rose |

1. _____

2. _____

3. _____

4. _____

WHILE YOU WATCH

2 Watch the video. Are the sentences true (T) or false (F)? Correct the false sentences.

1. _____ Monterrey is a big city in Mexico.   _____

2. _____ Priscilla is at school with her sister.   _____

3. _____ School finishes at three o'clock.   _____

4. _____ Priscilla plays water polo after school
              on Mondays and Thursdays.   _____

5. _____ Priscilla is 16 today.   _____

3 Watch the video again. Complete the sentences.

1. Girls always wear a special _____ to their party.

2. Parents give a special _____ to their daughter at the party.

3. Priscilla first dance is with her _____.

4. Priscilla father, brother, and grandfather give her a _____.

5. At the end of the party, Priscilla _____ with her friends.

AFTER YOU WATCH

4 Work in small groups. Discuss: How do you celebrate your birthday?

> I have a party on my birthday. My friends come to the party. We play games and we eat cake and ice cream.

Kung Fu SCHOOL

BEFORE YOU WATCH

1 Match the words with the correct pictures.

| sword | fight | brick | stick |

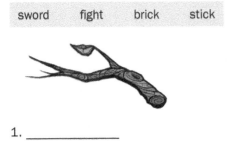

1. _____

2. _____

3. _____

4. _____

WHILE YOU WATCH

2 Watch the video. Complete the sentences with the correct adjectives.

| beautiful | famous | old | quiet |

Song Shan is a very ¹_____ town in the mountains. It's ²_____
and ³_____. It also has a ⁴_____ traditional kung fu school.

3 Watch the video again. Answer the questions.

1. Where is Song Shan? _____

2. Who is Master Li Yu? _____

3. What do the students do each morning? _____

4. What do the students fight with? _____

5. How many boys study at the school? _____

6. What time do they eat lunch? _____

7. Students at the school learn to fight. What else do they learn? _____

AFTER YOU WATCH

4 Work with a partner. What sports do the students at your school play? Make a list. What are your two favorites?

Students at my school play basketball, soccer, baseball, and tennis.
My favorites are basketball and baseball.

Tobilay's SCHOOL DAY

BEFORE YOU WATCH

1 Look at the picture from the video. Complete the sentences with the correct words.

netball   PE   South Africa

These students live in _____. They're in a _____ class. The name
of this sport is _____. It's similar to basketball.

WHILE YOU WATCH

2 Watch the video. Complete the sentences with the numbers.

5   8   14   300

1. Tobilay is _____ years old.

2. School starts at _____ o'clock.

3. The national song of South Africa has words from _____ languages in it.

4. The school makes lunch for _____ children.

3 Watch the video again. Number the events in the order that they happen from 1 to 6.

_____ Tobilay walks to school.

_____ The children learn traditional South African songs and dances.

_____ Tobilay plays netball with her classmates.

_____ Tobilay has class.

_____ The students eat lunch.

_____ Tobilay and the other students sing the national song.

FTER YOU WATCH

**4 Write about your day at school. What do you like doing? What don't you like doing? How is your day different
from Tobilay's day?**

School starts at 8:00 o'clock. I usually have English class first . . .

_____

Fishing IN JAPAN

BEFORE YOU WATCH

1 Look at the pictures from the video. Complete the sentences with the correct words.

to catch

a fisherman

an island

tuna

1. _____ is a very big fish.

2. _____ works on a boat.

3. _____ has water on all sides.

4. A fisherman's job is _____ fish.

WHILE YOU WATCH

2 Watch the video. Check [✔] the sentences you hear.

1. This is Japan, a country with thousands of islands. _____

2. These women are very young. _____

3. Fish is really good for you. _____

4. It's also difficult to catch! _____

5. The tuna is really happy. _____

3 Watch the video again. Circle the correct answers.

1. One-fifth of Japanese people are more than _____ years old.

   a. 55   b. 65   c. 75

2. The women find healthy _____ in the ocean.

   a. exercise   b. food   c. vegetables

3. Tuna is a very _____ fish in Japan.

   a. active   b. dangerous   c. popular

4. Osamu is very _____.

   a. fast   b. strong   c. tired

AFTER YOU WATCH

4 Complete the chart with your own information. Discuss: How often do you eat these foods?

Food	Once a week	Often (2–6 times a week)	Every day	Never
Vegetables			✗	
Rice / Pasta / Bread			✗	
Fish	✗			
Meat		✗		
Dessert				✗

> I eat vegetables and rice every day. I often eat fruit and meat. I eat fish once a week. I never eat dessert!

Dabbawallas

BEFORE YOU WATCH

1 Look at the pictures from the video. Match them with the correct words.

| dabbawalla | lunchbox | Mumbai | traffic |

1. _____ 2. _____ 3. _____ 4. _____

2 Complete the sentences with the words from Exercise 1.

1. _____ is a big city in India.

2. Big cities always have a lot of _____.

3. A _____ takes lunch to people in India.

4. People put food for lunch in a _____.

WHILE YOU WATCH

3 Watch the video. When do you see these things? Write numbers 1 to 5.

1. _____ A man on a bicycle

2. _____ A man in a kitchen

3. _____ A map of Mumbai

4. _____ A man in an office building

5. _____ A lunchbox with rice

4 Watch the video again. Circle the correct answers.

1. The girl's **brother / cousin** works in Mumbai.

2. He takes **lunch / breakfast** to people.

3. A lot of people in India like **hot / cold** food for lunch.

4. There are about **4,000 / 40,000** dabbawallas in the city.

5. The job is **easy / dangerous**.

AFTER YOU WATCH

5 Work with a partner. Take turns asking and answering the questions.

Where do you eat lunch?

What do you usually eat?

Who makes your food?

What is your favorite lunch?

I usually eat lunch in the cafeteria at my school.

Shark ATTACK!

BEFORE YOU WATCH

1 Look at the pictures from the video. Match the words with the definitions.

a.

shark

b.

submarine

c.

bite

1. to cut with your teeth _____

2. an underwater boat _____

3. a fish with very sharp teeth _____

WHILE YOU WATCH

2 Watch the video. When do you see these things? Write numbers 1 to 4.

_____ A shark biting a man

_____ A submarine going into the ocean

_____ A Greenland shark

_____ A Hammerhead shark

3 Watch the video again. Answer the questions about the Greenland shark.

1. In what ocean do the Greenland sharks live? _____

2. About how long can they be? _____

3. What kind of water do they like? _____

4. How deep can they go in the ocean? _____

5. How well do they see? _____

6. What kind of teeth do they have? _____

AFTER YOU WATCH

4 Work in small groups. Take turns describing different animals and guessing the names of the animals.

It is usually green. It lives in water. It can jump.

Is it a frog?

Animals IN THE CITY!

BEFORE YOU WATCH

1 Look at the pictures from the video. Match them with the correct words.

| camel | cow | elephant | horse | monkey | snake |

1. _____

2. _____

3. _____

4. _____

5. _____

6. _____

WHILE YOU WATCH

2 Watch the video. Circle the correct words.

1. There are a lot of **cats / rats** in the temple.

2. The rats eat **bananas / nuts**.

3. The rats drink **water / milk**.

4. In India, people think rats are **dangerous / special**.

5. People often **feed / eat** snakes in India.

6. At the end of the video, we see two men with two **snakes / elephants**.

3 Watch the video again. Are the sentences true (*T*) or false (*F*)? Correct the false sentences.

1. _____ More than a billion people live in India.

   _____

2. _____ There are more than 500 types of wild animals in this country.

   _____

3. _____ You can see camels and elephants in cities in India.

   _____

4. _____ People give milk with a little bit of honey to the rats.

   _____

5. _____ There is a camel festival in the town.

   _____

FTER YOU WATCH

4 Work in small groups. Discuss: What animals live in cities in your country? Who takes care of these animals?

> A lot of people have dogs in their homes. People take care of their pets.

Rome: ANCIENT AND MODERN

BEFORE YOU WATCH

1 Match the words with the definitions.

1. ancient _____
2. amphitheater _____
3. museum _____
4. modern _____

a. from the present

b. a place to see art and learn about history

c. from a long time ago

d. a place for games in ancient Rome

WHILE YOU WATCH

2 Watch the video. Are the sentences true (*T*) or false (*F*)? Correct the false sentences.

1. _____ There were theaters and markets and restaurants in ancient Rome.

_____

2. _____ Sometimes people died in the fights in the Colosseum.

_____

3. _____ People watch sports in the Colosseum today.

_____

4. _____ Many modern stadiums are similar to the Colosseum.

_____

3 Watch the video again. Circle the correct answers.

1. More than **3 million / 2 million** people visit Rome every year.

2. Even **3,000 / 2,000** years ago Rome was an important city.

3. About **1 million / 2 million** people lived in ancient Rome.

4. There were sometimes **1,000 / 10,000** people in the baths of ancient Rome at the same time.

5. There were about **50,000 / 5,000** people in the Colosseum in ancient Rome for every fight.

AFTER YOU WATCH

4 Work with a partner. Talk about a city near you. What can you do there? Where do you do it?

Where can I ride a bike?

You can go to the park.

Crossing CITIES

BEFORE YOU WATCH

1 Look at the pictures from the video. Match the kinds of transportation with the pictures.

1. _____

2. _____

3. _____

4. _____

a. Bullet Train   c. rickshaws

b. airplane   d. bus

WHILE YOU WATCH

2 Watch the video. Answer the questions with the correct words.

Beijing	India	Japan	Mumbai	Tokyo

1. What is the first city you see? _____

2. What country has rickshaws? _____

3. What city has cows in the streets? _____

4. What country is famous for its bullet trains? _____

5. In what city do a lot of people take planes to get to work? _____

3 Watch the video again. Circle the correct answers.

1. More than **20 million / 22 million** people live in Beijing.

2. There are about **50 million / 5 million** cars in Beijing.

3. People usually travel long distances by **train / bus** in Mumbai.

4. **Beijing / Tokyo** is the largest city in the world.

5. The Bullet Train travels at **300 / 330** kilometers per hour.

FTER YOU WATCH

4 Work in small groups. Discuss: Where do you go on weekdays? On weekends? How do you travel? How long does it take?

> I usually take the bus to school. It takes about 20 minutes.

The PALIO

BEFORE YOU WATCH

1 Complete the sentences with the correct words.

Siena   Palio   horse   years

1. The _____ is a very special event.

2. _____ is a city in the north of Italy.

3. It started about 700 _____ ago, in the Middle Ages.

4. Ten riders from ten different areas of the city compete in the _____ race.

WHILE YOU WATCH

2 Watch the video. Complete the paragraph with the correct words.

On the day of the race, there was a big parade. A lot of people
¹_____, the tradition of the Palio together.
People ²_____ up in clothes from the Middle
Ages and ³_____ traditional music. The parade
⁴_____ at the track in Siena's central square.
Everybody was excited. We ⁵_____ for the race
to begin.

3 Watch the video again. Answer the questions.

1. How often did Alberto practice for the race?

_____

2. How long is the race?

_____

3. What terrible thing happened in the race?

_____

4. What did people do at the end of the race?

_____

AFTER YOU WATCH

4 Work with a partner. Take turns asking and answering questions about an exciting game or celebration.

When was it?   Who was in it?

Where was it?   What happened?

I went to a professional basketball game. It was really exciting!

When was it?

Last month.

The BOWLER

BEFORE YOU WATCH

1 Look at the pictures from the video. Complete the sentences with the correct words.

batter

bat

bowler

cricket

sign language

These boys are playing ¹_____. In this game,
the ²_____ throws the ball and the ³_____
hits it with a ⁴_____. This man is deaf. He cannot hear.
He uses ⁵_____ to communicate.

WHILE YOU WATCH

2 Watch the video. Are the sentences true (*T*) or false (*F*)? Correct the false sentences.

1. _____ Fahimuddin is 22 years old.   _____

2. _____ Fahimuddin wants to be a professional
   baseball player.   _____

3. _____ He can throw the ball over 160 kilometers
   an hour.   _____

4. _____ He played cricket with his seven brothers as
   a child.   _____

5. _____ He can't see very well.   _____

3 Watch the video again. Answer the questions.

1. When did cricket start? _____

2. Where did cricket start? _____

3. How does Fahimuddin communicate? _____

4. What does a bowler do? _____

AFTER YOU WATCH

4 Work with a partner. Who are two of your favorite professional athletes? Why?

My favorite athlete is David Ortiz. He plays baseball. He's a very good batter.

City OF WATER

BEFORE YOU WATCH

1 Look at the pictures from the video. Complete the sentences.

canals in Venice

a gondola on a foggy day

masks for Carnevale in Venice

1. Venice has many streets of water called _____.

2. This is a special boat called a _____.

3. It's often hard to see in Venice because it's _____.

4. _____ is a big festival in Venice.

5. People wear amazing _____ at the festival.

WHILE YOU WATCH

2 Watch the video. Circle the correct answers.

1. Every day **16,000 / 60,000** people visit this city of water.

2. Venice is a city of **118 / 180** islands.

3. There are **170 / 177** canals in Venice.

4. The first Carnevale in Venice was in **1062 / 1162**.

5. There are **500 / 5,000** people at one of the parties!

3 Watch the video again. Complete the sentences.

1. Venice is in the northwest of _____.

2. The city is a group of _____.

3. There are no _____ in Venice.

4. Venetian _____ are very narrow boats.

5. People celebrate Carnevale in month of _____.

6. People wear _____ over their faces.

AFTER YOU WATCH

4 Work in small groups. Discuss: What are some special events in your country? Do you dress up in costume for any celebrations or festivals?

> I love St. Patrick's Day! Every year, I dress up in green clothes and only eat green food. Sometimes, I paint my hair green, too!

Alaska!

BEFORE YOU WATCH

1 Look at the pictures from the video. Complete the sentences with the correct words.

glacier   parachute   kayak

1. A _____ is a piece of equipment for jumping out of airplanes.

2. A _____ is a huge mountain of snow and ice.

3. People often use a _____ to explore rivers and lakes.

WHILE YOU WATCH

2 Watch the video. Circle the correct answers.

1. Alaska is next to _____.
   a. the United States   b. Canada   c. New York

2. Alaska is the _____ state in the United States.
   a. warmest   b. biggest   c. driest

3. The man is going to parachute over _____.
   a. rivers   b. beaches   c. glaciers

4. He's also going to _____ down some rivers.
   a. kayak   b. parachute   c. ski

5. He's going to _____ at night.
   a. see the Northern Lights   b. ski down icy mountains   c. camp by a river

3 Watch the video again. When do you see these things? Write numbers 1 to 5.

_____ skiing

_____ parachuting

_____ camping

_____ the Northern Lights

_____ kayaking

AFTER YOU WATCH

4 Work with a partner. Plan a four-day vacation. Describe where you're going to stay, what you're going to do, and what the weather is going to be like. Share your plans with the class.

> We're going to go to New York. We're going to stay in a hotel in Times Square. We're going to visit the Empire State Building.

Notes